Called by the Composer

Devotions for Musicians

Nancy Bell Kimsey

Published by Pine Warbler Publications
Fuquay-Varina, North Carolina, United States of
America

First Printing, 2023

Cover Art by Savannah Battle
Cover Design by Nathan Stikeleather

ISBN #9781736773147 (eBook)
ISBN #9781736773154 (Paperback)

To Erin and Megan:
You bring my heart overflowing joy.

I Can't...I've Got Rehearsal

And now, Israel, what does the LORD your God ask of you but to fear the LORD your God, to walk in obedience to him, to love him, to serve the LORD your God with all your heart and with all your soul, and to observe the LORD's commands and decrees that I am giving you today for your own good? Deuteronomy 10:12-13

Anyone who has ever made a serious commitment to a musical group knows that one result of this loyalty will be having to decline many invitations. Sporting events, slumber parties, volunteer opportunities – turned down because "I've got rehearsal." Sometimes we are secretly thankful for a credible way to get out of an undesirable event. In other situations, there is a great deal of sadness when we have to honor our duty to the group. So why make the sacrifice? We are motivated by our love of music and the joy that comes from working together to achieve a goal.

Following the commands of God and serving the Lord also involve sacrifice. We will need to relinquish time and resources. There will be occasions when we can't go along with the crowd. Friends or family may not understand our motivations. Yet we delight in the joys of fellowship and of working toward common goals.

Jesus is our example in sacrifice: *Who, being in very nature God, did not consider equality with God something to be used to his own advantage; rather, he made himself nothing by taking the very nature of a servant, being made in human likeness. And being found in appearance as a man, he humbled himself by becoming obedient to death–even death on a cross!* (Philippians 2:6-8)

Our service should always be motivated by love for God and for others, rather than by obligation: *to walk in obedience to him, to love him, to serve the LORD your God with all your heart and with all your soul.* (Deuteronomy 10:12) ...*love one another deeply, from the heart.* (1 Peter 1:22)

When I was a member of the marching band, I sometimes resented giving up the freedom to sit with non–band friends during games, wearing fashionable clothes instead of an awkward band uniform. So my senior year, I switched from band to chorus. I soon learned that a football game is ten times more fun when you experience it with a like–minded group of musicians! In the same way, when we love God and enjoy the fellowship of other believers, we will experience deep joy, even in situations that involve difficult sacrifice.

Prayer for Today:

Dear God, thank you for your great sacrifice on my behalf and for the true joy of serving you alongside others. I want to serve you cheerfully, even if I am misunderstood or weary, not from obligation but out of love for you. Amen.

Waiting in the Wings

I have no greater joy than to hear that my children are walking in the truth. 3 John 1:4

Would you volunteer to work backstage as a parent volunteer during a musical theatre show, knowing that you would miss the overall view of your own child's performance from the audience? I would, every time. While waiting in the wings I would have an amazing vantage point. I'd hear nervous giggles, see faces shining with excitement, and help with last–minute costume adjustments. Knowing what goes on backstage and sharing those special experiences with my child would make her moment of entrance onstage more thrilling and the completion of a successful performance more meaningful.

A teacher who directs a production from the wings wouldn't have a family bond with the actors. Still, there would be joy and satisfaction to see the long hours of rehearsal result in an experience that the students will always remember.

The Book of 3 John is a brief letter written to his friend Gaius, a faithful believer who has been like a spiritual child to John. He commends Gaius, saying, *It gave me great joy when some believers came and testified about your faithfulness to the truth, telling how you continue to walk in it. I have no greater*

3

joy than to hear that my children are walking in the truth.
(3 John 1:3-4)

The apostle Paul was used in a special way in the life of Timothy, whom he called *my dear son* (2 Timothy 1:2). Paul challenged him, *Don't let anyone look down on you because you are young, but set an example for the believers in speech, in conduct, in love, in faith and in purity.* (1 Timothy 4:12) *What you heard from me, keep as the pattern of sound teaching, with faith and love in Christ Jesus.* (2 Timothy 1:13)

It brings amazing happiness when our children thrive and grow into kind, accomplished human beings, but the greatest joy as a parent comes when our children demonstrate a growing relationship with God. Now consider this question: Are there any individuals that you are guiding as spiritual children? This could take the form of organized mentoring, but just as likely it might involve making a subtle but conscious effort to live before them in integrity and godliness, using the truth of Scripture as your guide. You wouldn't need to be perfect yourself – just a willing volunteer in the service of the Father. Being a part of the "backstage" of their lives will solidify your relationship and bring great blessing as these individuals grow in the grace and knowledge of the Lord Jesus Christ.

Prayer for Today:

Dear God, if you can use me to help someone draw closer to you, please make this clear to me. Show me how to honor you in my own life, and may I consider it a privilege to invest in the lives of others for the benefit of all and for your glory. Amen.

Talent Show

You are the light of the world. A town built on a hill cannot be hidden. Neither do people light a lamp and put it under a bowl. Instead they put it on its stand, and it gives light to everyone in the house. In the same way, let your light shine before others, that they may see your good deeds and glorify your Father in heaven.
Matthew 5:14-16

There's nothing like a middle school talent show audition. The vast majority of the hopefuls will be piano players, comedy groups with dubious levels of humor, and singers upon singers. I once was in charge of an audition at which four separate young ladies all insisted that they wanted to sing the theme from *Titanic*. Sigh…

There were probably many kids who never even auditioned for the show who were actually quite talented. There could have been many valid explanations for their disinterest: fear of performing, low opinion of their own talents, lack of time, or a negative experience in a similar production. No matter the reason, the audience likely missed the opportunity to hear some accomplished entertainers.

On the other hand, a talent show composed solely of prima donnas would also cause some people to miss out. The rank and file performers would miss the enjoyment of playing their parts with enthusiasm. The shy children who overcome stage fright would miss the opportunity to conquer their fears. The proud parents of a child who will never attend Juilliard but truly loves music would miss seeing that child's beaming face at the curtain call. Audience members would miss the experience of a fun, if rather chaotic, evening.

God gives many different types of talents and spiritual gifts to his people. *There are different kinds of gifts, but the same Spirit distributes them. There are different kinds of service, but the same Lord. There are different kinds of working, but in all of them and in everyone it is the same God at work.* (1 Corinthians 12:4-6) If I neglect to use my gifts out of fear, lack of confidence, or past difficulties, the greater body of Christ will miss out. If I wait to get involved because I view others in the group as being more gifted than myself, the body misses out. And if I herald my own skills in a way that discourages others from participating, the body also misses out. *Now to each one the manifestation of the Spirit is given for the common good.* (1 Corinthians 12:7)

Prayer for Today:

Dear God, you have given me gifts, and you have called me to use them for the common good. When I feel afraid or inadequate, help me to move forward in faith. Help me also to encourage those around me to get involved in the great work to which you have called us together. Amen.

A Harmonic Life

Peace I leave with you; my peace I give you. I do not give to you as the world gives. Do not let your hearts be troubled and do not be afraid.
John 14:27

Musical harmony is a creation of God. Our minds and hearts have an innate response to harmonic sounds. Many of us find ourselves automatically harmonizing to tunes that we hear on the radio. Constant dissonance, or even a long series of random notes, can feel stressful. In a wider sense, when our lives are in harmony with God and with others, we experience peace.

True inner peace begins by finding peace with God. *Therefore, since we have been justified through faith, we have peace with God through our Lord Jesus Christ, through whom we have gained access by faith into this grace in which we now stand.* (Romans 5:1-2) Peace is a result of the Holy Spirit dwelling inside of us. *But the fruit of the Spirit is love, joy, peace, forbearance, kindness, goodness, faithfulness, gentleness and self–control.* (Galatians 5:22-23)

God's peace can prevail even in difficult situations. *And the peace of God, which transcends all understanding, will guard*

your hearts and your minds in Christ Jesus. (Philippians 4:7)
*You will keep in perfect peace those whose minds are steadfast,
because they trust in you.* (Isaiah 26:3)

Peace is more likely when we follow the Lord's commands.
*Great peace have those who love your law, and nothing can
make them stumble.* (Psalm 119:165)

Peace can be pursued in very specific ways. (Attaining
peace, especially peace with others, is not just some vague
process of acquisition over time.)

*Let us therefore make every effort to do what leads to peace
and to mutual edification.* (Romans 14:19)
*If it is possible, as far as it depends on you, live at peace with
everyone.* (Romans 12:18)
*Also, seek the peace and prosperity of the city to which I have
carried you into exile.* (Jeremiah 29:7)
*Discipline your children, and they will give you peace; they
will bring you the delights you desire.* (Proverbs 29:17)
*Blessed are the peacemakers, for they will be called children of
God.* (Matthew 5:9)

Prayer for Today:

Dear Jesus, You are the Prince of Peace.
Thank you for paying the penalty for my sins
so that I can have peace with God. May your
Holy Spirit redesign my heart and life so that I
can experience peace with myself and others,
and may I put forth the effort needed to aid the
Spirit's work. Amen.

8

Golden Bowl or Clay Pot?

"Everyone who confesses the name of the Lord must turn away from wickedness." In a large house there are articles not only of gold and silver, but also of wood and clay; some are for special purposes and some for common use. Those who cleanse themselves from the latter will be instruments for special purposes, made holy, useful to the Master and prepared to do any good work. 2 Timothy 2:19-21

It's possible to buy a violin online for less than $100 or to purchase a rare European violin for over a million dollars. Many differences between the two instruments would be obvious at first glance. The expensive violin would have superior materials and construction. Other differences would only become apparent when each is played. The tone, resonance, and ease of playing the fine instrument all increase its value. In addition, the value of the violin can be increased exponentially if its maker has a history of extraordinary craftsmanship. A costly violin would likely be insured and protected from harm, and used for special performances.

In 2 Timothy, Paul uses the metaphor of household dishes to describe those who follow Christ. Some containers, those made of wood and clay, were used for everyday purposes such as storing water. Others vessels made of silver and gold would only have been used only on special occasions, in the same way that we bring out the "good china" for a holiday dinner. Paul explains, *Those who cleanse themselves from the latter* (the wickedness he has described earlier in the chapter) *will be instruments for special purposes, made holy, useful to the Master and prepared to do any good work.* (2 Timothy 2:21) Everyone who believes in Christ can be used by God in some way, but when sin is cleared from our lives we are available to be used for any good work, even for unique ministry tasks. What is the process for becoming a cleansed vessel?

First, ask God for awareness. *But who can discern their own errors? Forgive my hidden faults.* (Psalm 19:12)

Second, we must confess. *If we confess our sins, he is faithful and just and will forgive us our sins and purify us from all unrighteousness.* (1 John 1:9)

Third, study God's Word consistently. *The statutes of the LORD are trustworthy, making wise the simple. Keep your servant also from willful sins; may they not rule over me.* (Psalm 19:7, 13)

Finally, recognize that your Creator, the master craftsman, will continue to work in your life as you are open to his leading: *being confident of this, that he who began a good work in you will carry it on to completion until the day of Christ Jesus.* (Philippians 1:6)

Prayer for Today:

Dear God, you created me and you know all about me. Purify me through the truth of your Word. Give me an openness to be used for special purposes and the righteousness that will make me more useful to you. Amen.

Alumni Tradition

When you enter the land that the LORD will give you as he promised, observe this ceremony. And when your children ask you, "What does this ceremony mean to you?" then tell them, "It is the Passover sacrifice to the LORD, who passed over the houses of the Israelites in Egypt and spared our homes when he struck down the Egyptians." Then the people bowed down and worshiped. Exodus 12:25-27

Many high school and college choral groups have a tradition by which any choral alumni present at the holiday concert in December are invited to come up on stage for the final number. They join the current choir members for a familiar, much–loved song. This strikes a nostalgic chord among the parents, and the alumni usually enjoy participating in the number. But even more important than those benefits, this custom gives both the students and the audience a sense of being a part of something important and ongoing. They join a long line of families who have participated in this experience, and the tradition will continue even after all the students present on that evening have grown and moved away.

Our core beliefs are only one generation away from being lost if nothing specific is done to pass them on. *After that whole generation had been gathered to their ancestors, another generation grew up who knew neither the LORD nor what he had done for Israel.* (Judges 2:10) The people of Israel were instructed to carefully instruct their children and grandchildren in the faith. *Only be careful, and watch yourselves closely so that you do not forget the things your eyes have seen or let them fade from your heart as long as you live. Teach them to your children and to their children after them.* (Deuteronomy 4:9)

One method of spiritual instruction was the observance of particular ceremonies and rituals. In Leviticus 23, the Lord gives directions to Moses for the Passover, the Festival of Unleavened Bread, the Festival of Weeks, and other sacred assemblies that are to be observed by all the generations to come. The Sabbath is also included in this set of instructions to Moses, so we know that it is important to pass on the habit and privilege of Sabbath observance.

Little ones who are part of our sphere of influence are carefully watching us to see what we value. They will ask questions about our lives, and it can be our joy to share with them the truths of Scripture and the traditions of worship.

Prayer for Today:

Dear God, there are children that I interact with who will become part of the next generation to honor and serve you. May I not be negligent in showing them, by loving words and gracious deeds, that you desire to be their Savior and Lord. Amen.

Composing a New Song

He put a new song in my mouth, a hymn of praise to our God. Many will see and fear the LORD and put their trust in him. Psalm 40:3

Composing a piece of music, whether it be a simple lullaby or an intricate symphony, usually begins with a little musical motif – a brief piece of a melody that has been making a home in your brain that you want to release into the world. As you continue to craft your musical work, you will add variations and contrasting elements to your basic tune. You'll also put in harmonies that fit the mood of your composition. The seed of your musical work grows into a complete piece that can be shared and performed.

God has new songs already prepared for the culmination of history. In Revelation 5, the throne room of heaven is described, with Jesus as the focus, surrounded by heavenly beings. *Then I saw a Lamb, looking as if it had been slain, standing at the center of the throne, encircled by the four living creatures and the elders... And they sang a new song, saying: "You are worthy to take the scroll and to open its seals, because you were slain, and with your blood you purchased for God persons from every tribe and language and people and nation. ..Worthy is the Lamb, who was slain, to receive power*

13

and wealth and wisdom and strength and honor and glory and praise!" (Revelation 5:6,9,12)

In Revelation chapter 15, we get a vision of those who have been victorious over evil. They are playing harps and singing another new song, this one containing phrases from three Old Testament books. *Great and marvelous are your deeds, Lord God Almighty. Just and true are your ways, King of the nations. Who will not fear you, Lord, and bring glory to your name? For you alone are holy. All nations will come and worship before you, for your righteous acts have been revealed.* (Revelation 15:3-4)

Kernels of truth from God's Word and snippets of a melody…these can be the start of a musical composition which proclaims the greatness of God. Our new song will be an outpouring of the gratitude of our heart, guided by the Holy Spirit. Now is a good time to declare his greatness, *speaking to one another with psalms, hymns, and songs from the Spirit. Sing and make music from your heart to the Lord.* (Ephesians 5:19)

It is also a good time to consider the songs we will sing in heaven. Meditate upon the attributes and deeds of God outlined in the songs found in Revelation chapters 5 and 15. There's no time like the present to rehearse the songs that God has composed for the future.

Prayer for Today:

Dear Lord Jesus, you are worthy to receive
power and wealth and wisdom and strength
and honor and glory and praise! Amen.

The Older Brother

*Meanwhile, the older son was in the field. When he came near the
house, he heard music and dancing. So he called one of the servants
and asked him what was going on. "Your brother has come," he
replied, "and your father has killed the fatted calf because he has him
back safe and sound." Luke 15:25-27*

    The story of the prodigal son is one of the most famous
parables ever told by the Lord Jesus. The prodigal is the
younger son who squanders his inheritance with debauchery,
then comes to his senses and returns to his father. The father
welcomes him with open arms and immediately orders a feast
to celebrate his son's return. It's interesting that immediately
preceding this parable, Christ promises that *there is rejoicing in
the presence of the angels of God over one sinner who repents.*
(Luke 15:10)

    We know that the father's love prompts him to forgive his
younger son and to shower him with gifts. The son receives
new clothing, and the fatted calf is killed to provide food for
the big party. Yet it is also true that the prodigal endured the
consequences of his disobedience, coming almost to the point
of starvation. In the same way, while our heavenly Father
promises to forgive if we repent and return to him, we still
must suffer the natural effects of our sinful choices.

15

The older brother doesn't share his father's elation. Big brother angrily refuses to join the party because he has spent years "doing the right thing" – at least outwardly – and has not been rewarded with a celebration. *"Look! All these years I've been slaving for you and never disobeyed your orders."* (Luke 15:29) He definitely has a point, but it's sad that he seems unable to rejoice over the safe return of his brother. Perhaps if he had first seen his brother's emaciated state, he might have realized that the brother had at least partially "paid his dues".. The firstborn son will continue to hold his position as future inheritor of the estate. *"My son,"* the father said, *"you are always with me, and everything I have is yours. But we had to celebrate and be glad, because this brother of yours was dead and is alive again; he was lost and is found."* (Luke 15:31-32)

When we arrive in heaven one day, we will be overwhelmed with its splendor, captivated by seeing the face of Christ, and thankful for God's grace that has allowed us to be there. We will likely encounter some people that we are surprised to see – individuals who came to faith in Christ years after we knew them, but we will be happy to celebrate their place in heaven along with our own. In the meantime, as we live on this earth, let's joyfully serve God and seek out the lost, lovingly helping them to understand the good news that their heavenly Father longs for their return.

Prayer for Today:

Dear God, your grace to me is undeserved.
Thank you for loving me and celebrating when
I turned to you. May I share the words of life
with others so that they also can know your
grace and forgiveness. Amen.

How Did I End Up Here?

To the Jews who had believed him, Jesus said, "If you hold to my teaching, you are really my disciples. Then you will know the truth, and the truth will set you free." John 8:31-32

A choir is rehearsing an a cappella piece. The accompanist plays the opening note for each part, then sits back to listen while the director leads the group. Some of the singers progress blissfully through the song with the incorrect assumption that the intonation is holding, but others begin to feel uncomfortable as they recognize that the pitches are gradually going flat. At the end of the piece, the director asks the accompanist to play the final chord. Ouch! Without the guidance of a piano accompaniment, the group has sunk almost a whole step from the original key.

Singing a cappella takes intense concentration and a good ear, because drifting out of tune can happen so gradually that the singers may not even notice until it is too late. In the same way, our attitudes and behavior can gradually drift away from God's best plan for us if we don't have a standard by which to measure. The changing social mores of popular culture will never be a good benchmark, and even the opinions of well–

meaning friends and family are also inadequate if they are not based on truth.

What's the best way to keep our lives from gradually sliding away from God's accurate view of reality? Just as singers must always keep pitch in their minds as they sing, seeking wisdom and truth is a day–by–day, moment–by–moment process. Proverbs 8 personifies wisdom as calling out to us for our own good: *Blessed are those who listen to me, watching daily at my doors, waiting at my doorway. For those who find me find life and receive favor from the LORD.* (Proverbs 8:34-35) Once we understand the truth, we must make small decisions each day to keep our lives in alignment with it. *Give careful thought to the paths for your feet and be steadfast in all your ways.* (Proverbs 4:26). Then we won't examine our lives one day and ask ourselves, "How did I end up here?"

Jesus said, "If you hold to my teaching, you are really my disciples. Then you will know the truth, and the truth will set you free." (John 8:31-32)

Prayer for Today:

Dear God, sometimes I think that I can successfully navigate this life on my own, but in reality I just drift away from righteousness and the freedom that comes from knowing and following the truth. Thank you that your Word has all that I need to keep me in tune with your perfect plan for me. Amen.

Playing it by Ear

There is a way that appears to be right, but in the end it leads to death.
Proverbs 14:12

Maybe you know someone who can play music by ear, able to reproduce tunes without the aid of sheet music or chord charts. The stereotype of an individual with this talent would be the lounge entertainer who can seamlessly play and sing almost any request from the audience. Others can create perfect harmonies as they sing along with the radio or lead a worship service. In each case, while they may be "playing it by ear" in terms of creativity, spontaneity, and personal musical skill, the musicians must still adhere to underlying musical principles in order to create beautiful, harmonic music.

Many people approach their spiritual life with the flawed assumption that they can "play it by ear". Perhaps they have some degree of an innate sense of right and wrong, and they hope that this will be sufficient to live their lives in a way that will ultimately please God. Maybe they feel God's presence in nature, and trust that these feelings will lead them into peace with God and with other humans. What are the fallacies in these approaches to life?

First, we discover that it's difficult, even impossible to do the right thing. Selfishness takes over, and we behave in ways that hurt others. Pride causes us to elevate ourselves in our own minds above our holy and awesome Creator.

Second, at the end of our lives, the question remains, "How good is good enough to please God and live eternally with Him?" Where would the cut–off point be? Most world religions are based on the idea that man is trying to please God, but those religions teach that man will never have assurance of his final spiritual state.

Third, human ideas of right and wrong have varied within historical and societal contexts. So what is the alternative to "playing it by ear" as we go through life?

When we cry out, *I have the desire to do what is good, but I cannot carry it out...Who will rescue me from this body that is subject to death?* (Romans 7:18, 24), the answer comes: *Thanks be to God, who delivers me through Jesus Christ our Lord!* (Romans 7: 25)

When we decide to reach out in faith, God promises: *For it is by grace you have been saved, through faith – and this is not from yourselves, it is the gift of God – not by works, so that no one can boast.* (Ephesians 2:8-9)

When we need unchanging truth to guide our lives, we can look to the Scriptures: *The grass withers and the flowers fall, but the word of our God endures forever.* (Isaiah 40:8)

Prayer for Today:

Dear God, I know that I have sinned against you in thought, word, and deed. I trust in your grace to make me right with you, because Jesus has given his life to bring forgiveness to me. I trust in your unchanging Word to guide me in the future. Amen.

Leading Man

The LORD does not look at the things people look at. People look at the outward appearance, but the LORD looks at the heart.
1 Samuel 16:7

The sixteenth chapter of 1 Samuel recounts the selection of David to be the future king of Israel. Samuel, a prophet and judge, has been told by God that one of the sons of Jesse will be the Lord's choice. Samuel travels to Bethlehem to be introduced to Jesse's family. An interesting side note: this chapter forms the background as to why Bethlehem is referred to as the town of David in Luke's Christmas narrative. *So Joseph also went up from the town of Nazareth in Galilee to Judea, to Bethlehem the town of David, because he belonged to the house and line of David.* (Luke 2:4)

At this point the narrative takes some surprising twists. Jesse first brings forth his eldest son, Eliab, to meet the prophet. This would be culturally appropriate, but Eliab is not selected by Samuel. *When they arrived, Samuel saw Eliab and thought, "Surely the LORD's anointed stands here before the LORD." But the LORD said to Samuel, "Do not consider his appearance or his height, for I have rejected him. The LORD does not look at the things people look at.*

(1 Samuel 16:6-7) It's clear that Eliab had a rather kingly appearance, but Samuel is instructed by God not to consider this when making his decision. Next comes a memorable verse of Scripture, as useful in our generation as it was in the days of ancient kings: *People look at the outward appearance, but the LORD looks at the heart.* (1 Samuel 16:7)

After this, Jesse calls forward more of his sons, but each time the Lord reveals to Samuel that these young men are not to be chosen as king. Finally, Samuel asks if Jesse has any more sons! Jesse reveals that there is indeed one more son, his youngest, who is off tending the sheep. When David is brought before Samuel, the prophet receives God's confirmation that this youngest son is to be anointed as the future king.

It's intriguing that the physical appearance of David is actually described in even more favorable terms than that of Eliab. *He was glowing with health and had a fine appearance and handsome features.* (1 Samuel 16:12) We find out later in this chapter that David will also develop great musical talent on the lyre and will become a brave warrior. Quite the leading man! Yet God has clearly used other criteria in his selection of David. David's many strengths will be an asset in his role as king, but nothing will be more critical than a heart which follows the Lord. *...the LORD has sought out a man after his own heart...* (1 Samuel 13:14).

Prayer for Today:

Dear God, my inclination is to notice the appearance of others and to concern myself too much with my own appearance. I know that I need to focus on cultivating a pure heart that loves and honors you so that I may be used in your service.   Amen.

Don't Forget the Spats

Finally, be strong in the Lord and in his mighty power. Put on the full armor of God, so that you can take your stand against the devil's schemes. Ephesians 6:10-11

A marching band uniform has many parts, all designed for a crisp, visible, coordinated look. If a band member forgets a hat, gloves, or the right color socks, the entire ensemble will have a sloppy appearance. In high school, my habit was to go through an organized mental checklist before leaving home on game day, starting with the crimson plume that adorned my hat, all the way down to the white spats that snapped over black shoes.

The Bible encourages us to complete a similar checklist as we head out into the world each day. We are to remind ourselves daily to *put on the full armor of God.* (Ephesians 6:11) Why do we need spiritual armor? *For our struggle is not against flesh and blood, but against the rulers, against the authorities, against the powers of this dark world and against the spiritual forces of evil in the heavenly realms.* (Ephesians 6:12)

Our armor is described in detail in Ephesians chapter six. The defensive armor includes many parts:

- the belt of truth
- the breastplate of righteousness
- the shoes of readiness that come from the gospel of peace
- the shield of faith
- the helmet of salvation

Our offensive weapon is God's Word – the sword of the Spirit. *For the word of God is alive and active. Sharper than any double–edged sword, it penetrates even to dividing soul and spirit, joints and marrow; it judges the thoughts and attitudes of the heart.* (Hebrews 4:12) Mentally "putting on" each of these items of spiritual protection will help us to be less vulnerable to deceptive teachings, evil individuals, discouragement, and personal sin. Let's take advantage of every bit of armor which God has provided for us.

Prayer for Today:

Dear Lord, the enemy of my soul constantly
tries to attack my faith and weaken my
testimony by leading me into disobedience and
discouragement. May I consciously take
advantage of every piece of the armor that you
have provided for my protection. Amen.

Unresolved Issues

I plead with Euodia and I plead with Syntyche to be of the same mind in the Lord. Yes, and I ask you, my true companion, help these women since they have contended at my side in the cause of the gospel... Philippians 4:2-3

Do you feel relieved when a dissonant chord is resolved? For those of us who are accustomed to western tonality, musical resolution generally provides a sense of satisfaction. In layman's terms, it feels like "going home". This is just a small measure of the sensation we feel when a tense human situation is resolved. When there are obvious disagreements between individuals, the comment is sometimes made, "The tension in the room was so thick I could cut it with a knife." It can almost feel hard to breathe in discordant conditions.

The church at Philippi included two women who found it difficult to agree with one another. Although the exact nature of their disagreement is not revealed in Scripture, and although these women had apparently served faithfully alongside Paul to spread and defend the faith, he finds it necessary to earnestly plead with the women to cease their arguments. Paul even asks an unnamed companion to help resolve the dispute. So despite the good that these ladies have accomplished, several centuries later when the names of Euodia and Syntyche are mentioned, most people just recall their inability to work together. Very sad, indeed!

Earlier in his letter, Paul has made a more general appeal for accord in the Philippian church. He reminds the Philippians of the underlying basis for unity among them as believers, and he outlines some steps that will help them to achieve it: *Therefore if you have any encouragement from being united with Christ, if any comfort from his love, if any common sharing in the Spirit, if any tenderness and compassion, then make my joy complete by being like–minded, having the same love, being one in spirit and of one mind. Do nothing out of selfish ambition or vain conceit. Rather, in humility value others above yourselves, not looking to your own interests but each of you to the interests of the others.* (Philippians 2:1-4)

When you have an unresolved issue, seek to compassionately and humbly find a solution. If necessary, ask an uninvolved party to help bring resolution and peace. Take comfort in Christ's love for all involved, and focus on what you share in the Spirit.

Prayer for Today:

Dear Lord, is there any unresolved situation
that I have ignored that is hindering your work
and causing stress for others? Make me aware
of it, and give me a humble attitude and a heart
of love as I move forward. Thank you that
Christ is the Prince of Peace. Amen.

26

Chiming In

My dear brothers and sisters, take note of this: Everyone should be quick to listen, slow to speak, and slow to become angry. James 1:19

Playing in a handbell choir requires intense concentration. Members must constantly think ahead to upcoming measures and be ready with the correct handbell in order to chime in just at the right beat. An incorrect entrance will disrupt the flow of the entire piece.

Have you ever found yourself in a conversation with someone and suddenly realized that you are not really listening to the other individual? Your mind is leaping ahead to the comment that you intend to make. Because your brain is busy formulating what you think will be the perfect statement, the other person's words and emotions become inconsequential to you. Not only can this lead to misunderstandings, but it can undermine healthy relationships and communication. It's also a symptom of pride to believe that what I have to say is so brilliant or important that I can slack off on truly listening to others.

The Bible encourages us to be *quick to listen, slow to speak, and slow to become angry.* (James 1:19) Our minds are not to be preoccupied solely with thoughts about ourselves. *In his pride the wicked man does not seek him; in all his thoughts there is no room for God.* (Psalm 10: 4) *Do nothing out of selfish ambition or vain conceit. Rather, in humility value others above yourselves, not looking to your own interests but each of you to the interests of the others.* (Philippians 2:3-4)

Christ is our example and the source of any humility that we are able to obtain. *In your relationships with one another, have the same mindset as Christ Jesus: Who, being in very nature God, did not consider equality with God something to be used to his own advantage; rather, he made himself nothing by taking the very nature of a servant, being made in human likeness. And being found in appearance as a man, he humbled himself by becoming obedient to death–even death on a cross! Therefore God exalted him to the highest place and gave him the name that is above every name, that at the name of Jesus every knee should bow, in heaven and on earth and under the earth, and every tongue acknowledge that Jesus Christ is Lord, to the glory of God the Father.* (Philippians 2: 5-11)

Prayer for Today:

Dear God, forgive me for those times that I
have exalted my own thoughts and ideas and
have not really been a sincere listener. May
there always be room in my thoughts for you
and for the needs and opinions of others.
Grant me a humble view of myself, and use me
as a helper and encourager. Amen.

Just Not Right for That Part

We have different gifts, according to the grace given to each of us. If your gift is prophesying, then prophesy in accordance with your faith; if it is serving, then serve; if it is teaching, then teach; if it is to encourage, then give encouragement; if it is giving, then give generously; if it is to lead, do it diligently; if it is to show mercy, do it cheerfully.
Romans 12:6-8

If several very talented actors audition for a role in a musical theater production, all but one will be rejected. The decision sometimes comes down to factors such as height, appearance, or vocal tone quality. When the casting director has assigned all the parts, the production can successfully proceed with a cast composed of individuals who are all well suited for their roles.

God has created you with unique talents and characteristics which prepare you for certain responsibilities and opportunities. When we discover a profession or a group of friends that are a good match for us, we feel comfortable and satisfied. We can feel even more fulfilled if we are open to specific roles of service within our faith community

Currently sitting on the sidelines of service? Not every need that you see is a specific call upon your life, but it's also important not to assume that someone else will take care of all those needs. Ask God to show you paths of service that fit you as an individual. There is great joy to be found in giving of yourself to others.

Imagine a world in which people joyfully volunteer (rather than leaders begging for workers.) Visualize belonging to organizations in which 10% of the members don't do 90% of the work. The Bible encourages us to serve joyfully and energetically. ...*If it is giving, then give generously; if it is to lead, do it diligently; if it is to show mercy, do it cheerfully.* (Romans 12:8) Be creative and open in your approach to avenues of service.

Prayer for Today:

Dear God, grant me a heart that is sincerely available for service. Show me where I fit into the church body, and help me to not let fear or laziness hinder me from finding the perfect role for me in your kingdom.

Grand Concert Venues

I have indeed built a magnificent temple for you, a place for you to dwell forever... But will God really dwell on earth? The heavens, even the highest heaven, cannot contain you. How much less this temple I have built! 1 Kings 8:13, 27

Have you ever had the privilege to perform at a famous venue? Perhaps it was a quirky coffeehouse where a popular artist has performed in the past. Maybe your performing group has stood on the stage of a renowned concert hall where the architecture, decor, and sheer size took your breath away. The venue made the performance memorable. Now imagine reenacting the grand venue performance at the edge of the Grand Canyon, or in total darkness with the Northern Lights above. The awesome beauty of God's incredible creation would lift the concert to unforgettable heights.

When Solomon dedicated the elaborate temple that God had instructed him to build, he acknowledged that no earthly structure could contain God. Yet in his prayer of dedication, he also declared a number of reasons why this temple would be important.

First, God had seen fit to fill the temple with his glory (in the form of a dark cloud), showing God's approval.

Second, God had fulfilled many specific promises to Solomon (and his late father David) in the process of building the temple. *LORD, the God of Israel, there is no God like you in heaven above or on earth below – you who keep your covenant of love with your servants who continue wholeheartedly in your way. You have kept your promise to your servant David my father; with your mouth you have promised and with your hand you have fulfilled it – as it is today.* (1 Kings 8:23-24)

Finally, the temple will be a place where the people of Israel can pray for forgiveness and blessing. *...when they turn back to you and give praise to your name, praying and making supplication to you in this temple, then hear from heaven and forgive the sin of your people Israel...* (1 Kings 8:33-34)

When the prayers of God's people are answered, the result will be that the surrounding nations will recognize that the Lord is the one true God. *...that he may uphold the cause of his servant and the cause of his people Israel according to each day's need, so that all the peoples of the earth may know that the LORD is God and there is no other.* (1 Kings 8:59-60)

Prayer for Today:

Dear God, your vast and beautiful creation is not large enough to contain your glory. Not even the most elaborate building on earth can approach your magnificence. Thank you that you hear the prayers of each one of us. May the place where I worship be filled with holiness of character and fervency of prayer so that the surrounding world may know, love, and serve the one true God. Amen.

Music Camp Romance

The LORD appeared to us in the past, saying: "I have loved you with an everlasting love; I have drawn you with unfailing kindness.
Jeremiah 31:3

It's inevitable…teens head off to a one week music camp at a college or conference center, and before the week ends, a few romances have been kindled. While these infatuations are generally brief, at the time they are blissfully intense for the couples. Why do music camp romances occur so often? The participants are at their most desirable: excited about the week's events, frequently away from their regular peer group, and definitely on the lookout for new company. The couple doesn't spend enough time together to discover annoying habits or face the scrutiny of parents.

On the other hand, the mighty God, the creator of the universe, knows everything about each of us. *You have searched me, LORD, and you know me. You know when I sit and when I rise; you perceive my thoughts from afar.* (Psalm 139:1-2) Despite knowing all our shortcomings, God's affection encompasses us continually. God reaches out to us in love. *Give thanks to the LORD, for he is good. His love endures forever.* (Psalm 136:1) How amazing that the eternal

God desires a personal relationship with us! What is needed for this to happen? First, we admit our sin to the one who already knows our authentic self. *If we claim to be without sin, we deceive ourselves and the truth is not in us If we confess our sins, he is faithful and just and will forgive us our sins and purify us from all unrighteousness.* (1 John 1:8-9) Next, we believe that Jesus came to earth and died to take the penalty for our sin so that God's judgement would be diverted from us. *But he was pierced for our transgressions, he was crushed for our iniquity; the punishment that brought us peace was on him, and by his woulds we are healed. We all, like sheep, have gone astray, each of us has turned to our own way; and the LORD has laid on him the iniquity of us all.* (Isaiah 53:5-6)

If summer romance partners could return to the same home town, they might have the opportunity to strengthen their bond through spending more time together. Our new relationship with God is one that will grow and deepen throughout our life as we learn more about God through reading the Bible, praying, and committing to fellowship with others. When doubts and questions arise, remember that God has promised that what has been revealed to us is enough for us to follow him in the way that we should. *The secret things belong to the LORD our God, but the things revealed belong to us and to our children forever, that we may follow all the words of this law.* (Deuteronomy 29:29)

Prayer for Today:

Dear God, you know all about me and you love
me. I want to draw closer to you and learn
more about you. Thank you that your Word,
the Bible, reveals all that I will need to follow
you completely.   Amen.

Joyful Songs

Worship the LORD with gladness; come before him with joyful songs.
Psalm 100:2

Songs of joy are the natural outpouring of a heart filled with joy. Let's recount the many reasons why we can have a joyful heart:

God himself is the source of our joy, even when circumstances are not happy. *Glory in his holy name; let the hearts of those who seek the LORD rejoice. (1 Chronicles 16:10)*

The Lord has helped us and has proven himself trustworthy. *The LORD is my strength and my shield; my heart trusts in him, and he helps me. My heart leaps for joy, and with my song I praise him.* (Psalm 28:7)

God's love is unfailing. *Satisfy us in the morning with your unfailing love, that we may sing for joy and be glad all our days.* (Psalm 90:14)

Obeying the commands of God leads to joy. *If you keep my commands, you will remain in my love, just as I have kept my Father's commands and remain in his love. I have told you this so that my joy may be in you and that your joy may be complete.* (John 15:10-11)

God's Word is understandable. It is our heritage that brings us joy. *They read from the Book of the Law of God, making it clear…Then all the people went away to eat and drink… to celebrate with great joy, because they now understood the words that had been made known to them.* (Nehemiah 8:8, 12) *Your statutes are my heritage forever; they are the joy of my heart.* (Psalm 119:111)

Jesus is risen from the dead and ever lives to intercede on our behalf. *So with you: Now is your time of grief, but I will see you again and you will rejoice, and no one will take away your joy.* (John 16:22)

Salvation brings joy. *The jailer brought them into his house and set a meal before them; he was filled with joy because he had come to believe in God – he and his whole household.* (Acts 16:34)

Heaven will be a place where our joy will continue to increase. *You make known to me the path of life; you will fill me with joy in your presence, with eternal pleasures at your right hand.* (Psalm 16:11)

Prayer for Today:

Dear God, My heart overflows with joy, and my lips will sing joyful praise to you for who you are and for all that you have done in my life. Amen.

The Blast of the Trumpet

For the Lord himself will come down from heaven, with a loud command, with the voice of the archangel and with the trumpet call of God, and the dead in Christ will rise first. After that, we who are still alive and are left will be caught up together with them in the clouds to meet the Lord in the air. And so we will be with the Lord forever.
1 Thessalonians 4:16-17

Trumpets are mentioned in over one hundred verses of the Bible. A few of the references are negative ones, such as Christ's condemnation in Matthew 6:2 of hypocrites who use trumpets to publicly announce the giving of their offerings. Generally, trumpets are utilized at important moments, such as going into battle, setting out on a journey, calling the people to assemble for times of rejoicing, causing the walls of Jericho to tumble, announcing a change in leadership, and celebrating the return of the Ark of the Covenant from the territory of the Philistines.

Perhaps the most important trumpet proclamation of all has yet to occur – the sudden announcement of the second coming of Christ. The Bible calls this *the last trumpet*, and details are given in 1 Corinthians 15 and 1 Thessalonians 4.

First, we learn that this landmark occasion will take place unexpectedly. *So you also must be ready, because the Son of*

Man will come at an hour when you do not expect him.
(Matthew 24:44)

Second, this trumpet blast will coincide with the appearance of Jesus and the sound of an angel. *For the Lord himself will come down from heaven, with a loud command, with the voice of the archangel and with the trumpet call of God...* (1 Thessalonians 4: 16)

Third, this event will be visible to all. *"Men of Galilee,"* they said, *"why do you stand here looking into the sky? This same Jesus, who has been taken from you into heaven, will come back in the same way you have seen him go into heaven."* (Acts 1:11) *"Look, he is coming with the clouds,"* and *"every eye will see him, even those who pierced him"* (Revelation 1:7)

Finally, at the moment when the trumpet sounds, those believers who have already died will instantly be changed so that they have new, imperishable bodies. Then the living believers will join them in the air. *...the dead in Christ will rise first. After that, we who are still alive and are left will be caught up together with them in the clouds to meet the Lord in the air. And so we will be with the Lord forever. Therefore encourage one another with these words.* (1 Thessalonians 4:16-18)

Knowing that Christ will return for us someday should give us hope for the future and prompt us to service today . As Paul counseled the Corinthians immediately after explaining the future return of Christ, *Therefore, my dear brothers and sisters, stand firm... Always give yourselves fully to the work of the Lord, because you know that your labor in the Lord is not in vain.* (1 Corinthians 15:58)

Prayer for Today:
Even so come, Lord Jesus! I want to purify
myself to be ready for your coming. Amen.

Don't Boast

Brothers and sisters, think of what you were when you were called.
Not many of you were wise by human standards; not many were
influential; not many were of noble birth. But God chose the foolish
things of the world to shame the wise; God chose the weak things of
the world to shame the strong. God chose the lowly things of this
world ... so that no one may boast before him. 1 Corinthians
1:26-29

Healthy self–esteem taken to the extreme becomes boasting. Musicians and athletes who boast of their talents and accomplishments often receive positive press, but only one acceptable reason for boasting is given in Scripture: proclaiming the awesome works of the Lord. The psalmist wrote, *In God we make our boast all day long, and we will praise your name forever.* (Psalm 44:8) In 1 Corinthians chapter 1, Paul reminds his readers that any righteousness that we have achieved is a gift from God through Jesus. *It is because of him that you are in Christ Jesus, who has become for us wisdom from God – that is, our righteousness, holiness and redemption. Therefore, as it is written: " Let the one who boasts boast in the Lord."* (1 Corinthians 30-31)

Paul describes the early church as being comprised mostly of average citizens, rather than "celebrity" congregants. *Not many of you were wise by human standards; not many were influential; not many were of noble birth.* (1 Corinthians 1:26) Do we sometimes wish that our church had some well known members whose visibility (and bank accounts) might bring positive attention to our little gathering? James warned his readers against showing favoritism to the wealthy: *If you show special attention to the man wearing fine clothes and say, "Here's a good seat for you," but say to the poor man, "You stand there" or "Sit on the floor by my feet," have you not discriminated among yourselves? ...Has not God chosen those who are poor in the eyes of the world to be rich in faith and to inherit the kingdom he promised those who love him?* (James 2:3-5)

Perhaps you don't favor the rich or even those who are wise in the perspective of the world. Maybe your boasting is confined to your own secret heart attitude that God has chosen you because you are a pretty good person. Nothing could be further from the truth. *For it is by grace you have been saved, through faith – and this is not from yourselves, it is the gift of God– not by works, so that no one can boast.* (Ephesians 2:8-9)

Love is patient, love is kind. It does not envy, it does not boast, it is not proud. It does not dishonor others, it is not self–seeking...(1 Corinthians 13:4-5)

Prayer for Today:

Dear God, you have forgiven and redeemed me in grace and mercy, not because of any good works that I have tried to do. Grant me an attitude of humility this day. Keep me from self–seeking, envy, and pride. Amen.

Family Support

*Just as a body, though one, has many parts, but all its many parts form
one body, so it is with Christ…If the whole body were an eye, where
would the sense of hearing be?…As it is, there are many parts, but
one body.*
1 Corinthians 12:12, 17, 20

The young violin player peers around the edge of the stage
curtain in her school auditorium, hoping to catch a glimpse of
her father. He's been away on a business trip, so she's not
certain that he will be able to get there in time. Yes! He made
it! Support from a family member means the world to her. She
scoots over to her best friend, who gives her a hug when she
hears the good news. More support!

After the concert, in the chaos of excited chatter, photos,
and flower bouquets, her perceptive teacher is on the lookout
for students whose support system isn't visible. She makes a
special effort to engage them in conversation and give
encouraging compliments.

Is your adult support system a bit thin at this time? Your
Heavenly Father is watching, and He cares for you. *How
precious to me are your thoughts, God! How vast is the sum of*

them! (Psalm 139:17) *Cast all your anxiety on him because he cares for you. (1 Peter 5:7)*

God also designed for us to live in fellowship with other believers. *But God has put the body together, giving greater honor to the parts that lacked it, so that there should be no division in the body, but that its parts should have equal concern for each other. If one part suffers, every part suffers with it; if one part is honored, every part rejoices with it. (1* Corinthians 12:24-26) What if you are currently out of fellowship because you have recently moved to a new city or are nursing hurts from past negative experiences in a group of believers? It can be very difficult to seek out a new group and settle into it, but it's valuable to push through the process of finding a new spiritual home so that you can be supported.

If you have others who currently encourage and challenge you, be thankful. Then look around you. There are many others who have no family nearby, no one who comes up to them at the beginning of a worship service, no one to follow up on a prayer request. This is your opportunity to really see that person and to reach out. Don't assume that someone else will do this. Both of you will benefit by sharing your joys and sorrows.

Prayer for Today:

Dear God, open my eyes to see those who could use my support. Help me to move past my timidity and lack of compassion, so that your body will function the way that you designed it. Amen.

Go, Horse, Go!

Do you give the horse its strength or clothe its neck with a flowing mane? Do you make it leap like a locust, striking terror with its proud snorting? ...In frenzied excitement it eats up the ground; it cannot stand still when the trumpet sounds. At the blast of the trumpet it snorts, "Aha!" It catches the scent of battle from afar...
Job 39:19-20, 24-25

Pep bands are great fun, but admittedly their repertoire is limited. An entire basketball game can elapse with the pep band playing only *The Star Spangled Banner,* a few popular rock tunes, a handful of movie soundtrack themes, and forty–one performances of the school fight song. But when the band does launch into the fight song, there is an immediate reaction from the cheerleaders and fans. Like Pavlov's dogs, the sound elicits a physical response as people leap to their feet and clap. Hopefully, the home team's players also find their senses awakened and their basketball skills sharpened! Otherwise, the presence of the pep band is pointless, except to make the game a bit more fun for all the attendees.

In Job chapters 38-41, God asks Job a series of questions that highlight the intricacies of God's creation, especially the appearance and habits of animals. God describes a mighty

43

horse in the heat of combat, snorting and pawing the ground, literally unable to remain still when it hears the trumpet signal to advance in battle. *In frenzied excitement it eats up the ground; it cannot stand still when the trumpet sounds.* (Job 39:24) The horse has an innate reaction to this stimulus. Humans also respond to various types of music by feeling excitement, tension, or sadness, depending on the genre. Specific songs that bring back a strong memory will also elicit an emotional response.

God created us with hearts and brains that respond to music, and for this we can be grateful. We can choose to surround ourselves with lyrics that are acceptable to God. We can produce melodies and rhythms that bring happiness and peace to others. We can use our musical talents with humility.

Music comes from God; use music to honor him.

Prayer for Today:

Dear God, your creation is amazing. You gave me a brain that can interpret sound and a heart that can respond to it. Thank you for giving me a particular love of music, and may that love lead to new avenues of service to you. Amen.

Fair Warning

Jesus replied, "Anyone who loves me will obey my teaching."
John 14:23

The prophet Ezekiel lived during the time of the
Babylonian captivity, a period in which God's rebellious
people had been exiled in order to bring them to a state of
repentance. His messages included grim predictions about the
fall of Jerusalem, hopeful promises about the restoration of
Israel to their own land, and visions that have yet to be fulfilled
in our day.

Ezekiel is told by the Lord that many of his listeners will
ignore his warnings and refuse to change their ways. They
display curiosity about the prophet and appreciate his style of
delivery, but fail to make alterations in their inner heart
attitudes or outward habits. *My people come to you, as they
usually do, and sit before you to hear your words, but they do
not put them into practice... Indeed, to them you are nothing
more than one who sings love songs with a beautiful voice and
plays an instrument well, for they hear your words but do not
put them into practice.* (Ezekiel 33:31-32)

Today, many people decide to join a particular church congregation because of the talents of the musicians, rather than carefully considering whether or not the pastor is accurately and fully declaring the truth of the Bible. Others only want to listen to sermons that make them feel good about themselves. *For the time will come when people will not put up with sound doctrine. Instead, to suit their own desires, they will gather around them a great number of teachers to say what their itching ears want to hear.* (2 Timothy 4:3) Still others hear warnings found in Scripture but push aside the voice of God as it tells them to make changes in their thoughts, goals, or actions.

Jesus cautioned his listeners: *Therefore everyone who hears these words of mine and puts them into practice is like a wise man who built his house on the rock... but everyone who hears these words of mine and does not put them into practice is like a foolish man who built his house on sand. The rain came down, the streams rose, and the winds blew and beat against that house, and it fell with a great crash.* (Matthew 7:24, 26)

May we echo the words of the psalmist: *Blessed are those who keep his statutes and seek him with all their heart...I have hidden your word in my heart that I might not sin against you... Give me understanding, so that I may keep your law and obey it with all my heart.* (Psalm 119:2, 11, 34)

Prayer for Today:

Dear God, give me insight into the truth of your Word and the deep desire to obey it. You promise great blessing to everyone who truly seeks you.   Amen.

46

Background Music

*Be still and know that I am God; I will be exalted among the nations,
I will be exalted in the earth. Psalm 46:10*

Piped in music is so commonplace today that we encounter it in stores, restaurants, elevators, airports, even storage units. Some of this music can be annoying, such as repetitive playlists of holiday tunes played for weeks on end. At other times, we are not consciously aware of the songs, because our brains have tuned them out.   Yet the music can still have its targeted effect, such as inducing calmness in an upscale restaurant or generating physical energy at a shopping mall. Many of us find it hard to endure periods of total silence, even as we prepare to worship God.   Yet this is what we are called to do. *The LORD is in his holy temple; let all the earth be silent before him.* (Habakkuk 2:20) Silence shows respect and helps to clear our minds of other thoughts.

Be still and know that I am God; I will be exalted among the nations, I will be exalted in the earth. (Psalm 46:10) It's important to note that this verse is found in the middle of a psalm that declares God's presence and help in the midst of natural disasters and wars. *God is our refuge and strength, an ever–present help in trouble. Therefore we will not fear,*

*though the earth give way and mountains fall into the heart of
the sea...Nations are in uproar, kingdoms fall...He says, "Be
still, and know that I am God"...The LORD Almighty is with
us; the God of Jacob is our fortress...* (Psalm 46:1-2, 6, 10, 11)
In times of turmoil, stopping to sit quietly before God is vitally
important.

*The LORD is my shepherd, I lack nothing. He makes me lie
down in green pastures, he leads me beside quiet waters, he
refreshes my soul.* (Psalm 23:1-2)

When our time of meditation and worship has ended, and
it's time to reenter the noise of the world, it's good to
remember that our own voices don't need to send forth
constant background noise to everyone around us. Chattering
around others isn't often helpful or appreciated. Perhaps you
know a soft–spoken individual who is well respected. When
that person speaks up, people listen. *The quiet words of the
wise are more to be heeded than the shouts of a ruler of fools.*
(Ecclesiastes 9:17)

Quietness is one of the effects of righteousness in a home or
in a nation. *Better a dry crust with peace and quiet than a
house full of feasting, with strife.* (Proverbs 17:1) *The LORD's
justice will dwell in the desert, his righteousness live in the
fertile field. The fruit of that righteousness will be peace; its
effect will be quietness and confidence forever.* (Isaiah
32:16-17)

Prayer for Today:

Dear Lord, you are the great and mighty God.
I silently wait before you. Amen.

Teachers Under the Microscope

Not many of you should become teachers, my fellow believers, because you know that we who teach will be judged more strictly. We all stumble in many ways. Anyone who is never at fault in what they say is perfect, able to keep their whole body in check. James 3:1-2

The book of James states that teachers will be judged more rigorously than others: "...we who teach will be judged more strictly." (James 3:1) All of us have certainly sat through classes with minds full of criticism regarding the words, idiosyncrasies, and even the physical appearance of our teachers. We who pursue a career in education find that when speaking aloud all day, there are inevitably words said that we wish we could take back, and so we long to be one "who is never at fault in what they say..." (James 3:2)

Why are teachers (whether educational or spiritual) judged more strictly? First, instructors are more visible than their students. Second, by leading the group, it's assumed that the teacher should be more knowledgeable and accomplished than the pupils. In the case of spiritual teachers, the lives of these individuals should be also morally above reproach. Finally, students are often critical just out of boredom, rudeness, or an elevated opinion of their own skills.

So why would anyone want to become a music director or teacher? The reasons are many:
- the satisfaction of pulling together a group of diverse musicians to make a beautiful, cohesive sound.
- the joy of helping individuals progress in their skills
- the privilege of spending the work day involved in what we love.

In Bible days, disciples would literally follow their teacher around, listening to the teacher's words and watching their leader's responses to the everyday situations of life. The critics of Jesus often asked him what they thought would be "gotcha" questions, but Jesus answered their judgmental and false inquiries with such wisdom that "no one dared to ask him any more questions." (Luke 20:40) His life was above reproach, and His teaching astounded his listeners. The disciples who were sincere seekers of truth followed Christ with open hearts that were willing to learn rather than to judge.

Prayer for Today:

Dear God, when you give me opportunities to teach, help me to be a faithful, honorable, inspiring instructor. When I stumble, teach me humility and grant to me your forgiveness. As a student of Jesus, help me to be an obedient, dedicated, and worshipful learner. Amen.

The Year of the Flutes

Suppose a man comes into your meeting wearing a gold ring and fine clothes, and a poor man in filthy old clothes also comes in. If you show special attention to the man wearing fine clothes and say, "Here's a good seat for you," but say to the poor man, "You stand there" or "Sit on the floor by my feet," have you not discriminated among yourselves and become judges with evil thoughts? (James 2:2-4)

In the late 1970's, our local school system set up several schools entirely composed of sixth graders as a way to transition into the middle school format. As a new teacher, I immediately learned that students would be assigned to our classes based on the band instrument they played, in order to pull out the beginning band students in small groups by instrument. The running joke among the teachers was that you did <u>not</u> want to be assigned the drummers or the trumpet players (lots of aggressive boys). A year with no band students was considered to be the worst assignment, as musicians overall were viewed as more motivated and disciplined individuals. I must admit that my year with the flutes was the most peaceful year I have ever experienced as an educator.

Some stereotypes do have a basis in reality, but we must be very careful not to pigeonhole people based on our previous experiences with a group to which that individual belongs. This is true for ethnicity, income level, profession, and many other defining characteristics. God chose to first share the message of the birth of the Messiah to a group of shepherds. In that culture, shepherds were viewed as unreliable, and their testimony was not accepted in court. By choosing the shepherds at this pivotal moment of history, God demonstrated his concern and respect for all.

Jesus warned his disciples to not judge anyone who entered the worship assembly based on clothing or perceived income level. In many of the parables of Jesus, the hero was a Samaritan (a group for which the Jews had great distaste.) God's love and mercy are available to all, and we must have hearts and minds that see each person as a unique individual who is cherished by the Creator.

Prayer for Today:

Dear God, I know that I often make judgements based on the groups to which certain people belong. Sometimes I'm not willing to share my life or communicate your love to those individuals. Forgive my sin, and change my outlook so that I can see people the way that you see them. Amen.

Seat of Honor

...whoever wants to become great among you must be your servant, and whoever wants to be first must be slave of all. For even the Son of Man did not come to be served, but to serve, and to give his life as a ransom for many." Mark 10:43-45

It doesn't take long for newbie sixth grade band members to realize that there is definitely a hierarchy within their respective sections. Once they have attained a basic ability to play their instruments, the director begins holding unannounced auditions to order them by skill level. The most accomplished player earns the right to play solos and sit in the first chair position as the obvious "top dog".

If a player's mother had gone to the director to ask that her child be placed in the seat of honor, the band members would have been indignant. Yet this is exactly what one mother asked of Jesus.

Then the mother of Zebedee's sons came to Jesus with her sons and, kneeling down, asked a favor of him. "What is it you want?" he asked. She said, "Grant that one of these two sons of mine may sit at your right and the other at your left in your kingdom." (Matthew 20:20-21) Jesus quickly shut down that inquiry, and later he reminded all of the disciples, *"whoever wants to become great among you must be your servant...just as the Son of Man did not come to be served, but to serve, and to give his life as a ransom for many."* (Matthew 20:26-28) Not only is Christ reminding them of the virtue of humility, but he is predicting that he will actually give up his own life to pay the penalty due all who have sinned. (Even for the sins of the mother who made the audacious request.)

Seating order was apparently very important in New Testament days. Jesus warned against emulating religious leaders who make a show of their piety and who crave attention. *...they love the place of honor at banquets and the most important seats in the synagogues...* (Matthew 23:6) Jesus noticed that wedding guests often tried to grab places of honor at a wedding banquet, so he gave this advice: *When someone invites you to a wedding feast, do not take the place of honor, for a person more distinguished than you may have been invited...But when you are invited, take the lowest place, so that when your host comes, he will say to you, "Friend, move up to a better place." Then you will be honored in the presence of all the other guests. For all those who exalt themselves will be humbled, and those who humble themselves will be exalted."* (Luke 14:8,10)

Prayer for Today:

Dear God, I know that each day I need a humble outlook on my sins and a joyful willingness to serve. May my actions and attitudes mirror your selfless life. Transform me by the working of your Holy Spirit. Amen.

Renaissance Man

God gave Solomon wisdom and very great insight…his fame spread to all the surrounding nations. He spoke three thousand proverbs and his songs numbered a thousand and five. He spoke about plant life, from the cedar of Lebanon to the hyssop that grows out of walls. He also spoke about animals and birds, reptiles and fish. From all nations people came to listen to Solomon's wisdom. 1 Kings 4:29, 31-34

A man who has been educated in a wide variety of cultural pursuits and areas of learning is sometimes called a Renaissance Man, and Leonardo da Vinci is frequently named as the embodiment of this term. In today's highly specialized culture, there seem to be fewer opportunities for individuals to study a wide range of topics in the arts and sciences. Even in athletics, young children are being encouraged to hone in on a single sport, often resulting in overuse injuries. But most scientists agree that there are clear intellectual and social benefits to studying music as a child, regardless of your interests and talents.

Solomon was a particularly well rounded man with expertise in plants, animals, administration, poetry, and music (the composer of one thousand and five songs!) But he is most remembered for his remarkable wisdom, given by God at

Solomon's own request. *The Lord was pleased that Solomon had asked for this... "Since you have asked for this and not for long life or wealth for yourself, nor have asked for the death of your enemies, but for discernment in administering justice, I will do what you have asked...Moreover, I will give you what you have not asked for – both wealth and honor – so that in your lifetime you will have no equal among kings."* (1 Kings 3:10-13) The Lord granted Solomon almost unfathomable wealth, in addition to the privilege of building the magnificent temple in Jerusalem.

What would be the skill set of a spiritual Renaissance man or woman? We're definitely not all called to be experts in teaching, evangelism, or even encouragement of others. But all of us should have a working knowledge of the Bible and be committed to understanding it more clearly. Everyone should be devoted to prayer and to the glad service of others. We should have discerning minds and hearts of love. And those of us that love music should use our talents to glorify God and encourage others.

Prayer for Today:

Dear God, it is my desire to please you in all things. I won't be a leader in every aspect of spiritual life, but this shouldn't keep me from studying your Word, serving others, praying, or any other activity to which you call me. I know that having a sincere heart of devotion to you is more important than any skill that I could cultivate. Please lead me with your wisdom and grant me joy each day. Amen.

The Musical Holding Pattern

Wait for the Lord; be strong and take heart and wait for the Lord.
Psalm 27:14

The actress in a musical theatre production misses her entrance because her quick costume change has been stalled due to a stuck zipper. The pit orchestra conductor signals the musicians to continue to vamp over and over until the actress reappears and the show can continue. But during the musical holding pattern the audience and cast members can soon become curious, then restless, and eventually stressed. Circling an airport without knowing why the plane can't land also inspires irritation or fear. In many circumstances, life situations seem to be stuck on repeat for no apparent reason, and we cry out to God, *How long, LORD, how long?* (Psalm 6:3)

God not only knows what we are going through, He also knows how and when our waiting will end. But practically speaking, what truths can we cling to during times when we feel as though we are slogging through swampy terrain on a circular path?

– God is good. *Taste and see that the Lord is good; blessed is the one who takes refuge in him.* (Psalm 34:8)

– God is just and justice wins in the end. *Yet the Lord longs to be gracious to you; therefore he will rise up to show you compassion. For the Lord is a God of justice. Blessed are all who wait for him!* (Isaiah 30:18)

– God is with me. *So do not fear, for I am with you; do not be dismayed, for I am your God. I will strengthen you and help you; I will uphold you with my righteous right hand.* (Isaiah 41:10)

– Jesus suffered and He understands. *For we do not have a high priest who is unable to empathize with our weaknesses, but we have one who has been tempted in every way, just as we are – yet he did not sin.* (Hebrews 4:15)

– God is our help in times of trouble. *God is our refuge and strength, an ever–present help in trouble.* (Psalm 46:1)

– I can look at creation for inspiration. *I lift up my eyes to the mountains – where does my help come from? My help comes from the Lord, the Maker of heaven and earth.* (Psalm 121:1-2)

Prayer for Today:

Dear God, You know all about my situation. Grace me peace as I wait, and bring about a just resolution that will lead to my good and to your glory. Help me to trust in your love and power today. Amen.

Portable Music

Sing and make music from your heart to the Lord, always giving thanks to God the Father for everything, in the name of our Lord Jesus Christ. Ephesians 5:19

Before there were playlists, there were harmonicas, ukuleles, mouth harps, and fifes for portable music. But the most portable instrument of all is the human voice. Whether you're standing on a mountain summit or a crowded subway, your voice is always available, but does it always honor God? Not every song we sing needs to have a religious theme, but our songs should never include questionable lyrics or tear others down. *With the tongue we praise our Lord and Father, and with it we curse human beings, who have been made in God's likeness. Out of the same mouth come praise and cursing. My brothers and sisters, this should not be.* (James 3: 9-10)

When in doubt, remember that as believers we are not bound by sets of legalistic rules, but we choose to put limits on our behavior because of our love for Christ and for one another. *"I have the right to do anything," you say – but not everything is beneficial. "I have the right to do anything" – but I will not be mastered by anything... Do you not know that your bodies are temples of the Holy Spirit, who is in you, whom you have received from God? ...Therefore honor God with your bodies.* (1 Corinthians 6: 12, 19-20)

To speak or sing in the name of Jesus means to use our voices in a way that would please Christ, and to seek the Lord's glory above all. *Sing and make music from your heart to the Lord, always giving thanks to God the Father for everything, in the name of our Lord Jesus Christ.* (Ephesians 5:19-20) *We pray this so that the name of our Lord Jesus may be glorified in you, and you in him, according to the grace of our God and the Lord Jesus Christ.* (2 Thessalonians 1:12)

The Bible mentions many kinds of songs, including songs of joy, thanksgiving, praise, even deliverance. Personal songs, like speech, are an outpouring of what is in our hearts. *For the mouth speaks what the heart is full of.* (Luke 6:45) Filling our hearts with songs and Scripture verses that remind us of God's faithfulness will enable us to call forth songs of encouragement when times are difficult. Music can also provide a meaningful way to pass on our faith to the next generation. *Only be careful, and watch yourselves closely so that you do not forget the things your eyes have seen or let them fade from your heart as long as you live. Teach them to your children and to their children after them.* (Deuteronomy 4:9)

Prayer for Today:

Dear God, I love you, and I'm so thankful for all your goodness to me. My desire is to honor you in my speech and my songs. Thank you that in every location and every circumstance, I may sing to you with a heart of worship. Amen.

The Jocks Get All the Perks

So many who are first will be last, and many who are last will be first
Matthew 19:30

At many high schools, athletes seem to command more adulation than musicians. Marching band rehearsals are held in a parking lot while the football team utilizes the field. Pep rallies are scheduled before the big game, not the big concert. There might be some measure of admiration for a great halftime routine, a show choir number, or a musical theatre production, but the applause can sometimes feel hard to come by. Musicians can feel like second class citizens.

The apostle Paul affirms the value of each individual to God in his letter to the Romans: *Very rarely will anyone die for a righteous person, though for a good person someone might possibly dare to die. But God demonstrates his own love for us in this: While we were still sinners, Christ died for us.* (Romans 5:7-8)

When we feel that our earnest desire to please God is not appreciated by others, we can remind ourselves that God knows and prizes our inner being. In the Old Testament, God revealed to Samuel, *the LORD does not look at the things*

61

people look at. People look at the outward appearance, but the LORD looks at the heart. (1 Samuel 16:7) Hagar spoke these words after the LORD encouraged her during a time of despair: *She gave this name to the LORD who spoke to her: "You are the God who sees me..."* (Genesis 16:13)

Perhaps you know that Jesus once said, *the last will be first, and the first will be last.* (Matthew 20:16) What is the context of this statement? Jesus has just finished interacting with a rich young man who turns away from an opportunity to follow Christ because he does not want to give up his current lifestyle. Jesus promises the disciples that He sees the heart and will reward those who have sacrificially followed Him.

Some takeaways from these verses:
- What the world esteems is often not what God values most highly. *And what does the LORD require of you? To act justly and to love mercy and to walk humbly with your God.* (Micah 6:8)
- God knows our heart, and He sees our service when no one else does. *As Jesus looked up, he saw the rich putting their gifts into the temple treasury. He also saw a poor widow put in two very small copper coins. "Truly I tell you," he said, "this poor widow has put in more than all the others."* (Luke 21:1-3)
- God is just, and justice will prevail in God's own timing. *Will not the Judge of all the earth do right?* (Genesis 18:25)

Prayer for Today:

Dear God, help me to remember that all I think, do, and say is known fully by you. May I faithfully serve you without concern for the recognition of others, trusting you to act justly. Amen.

The God of Creation

They exchanged the truth about God for a lie, and worshiped and served created things rather than the Creator – who is forever praised.
Romans 1:25

How many percussion instruments can you name? Most people could list several types of drums (snare drum, kettle drum, bass drum, etc.) as well as other members of the percussion family such as cymbals, marimba, chimes, triangle, wood block, tambourine, and even cowbell. Some sources list hundreds of instruments in the percussion family, if you include those from around the world. Percussion players truly have to be well rounded in their skills!

Now think of a category not made by humans, such as minerals. Naming quartz, silica, and tourmaline would only scratch the surface of the thousands of minerals that God created. *For this is what the LORD says – he who created the heavens, he is God; he who fashioned and made the earth.* (Isaiah 45:18) God's creativity and power are incomprehensible. *Can you bring forth the constellations in their seasons or lead out the Bear with its cubs? Do you know the laws of the heavens?* (Job 38:32-33) The creation is designed to teach us about God and to humble us before Him.

*For since the creation of the world God's invisible qualities –
his eternal power and divine nature – have been clearly seen,
being understood from what has been made, so that people are
without excuse.* (Romans 1:20)

The Book of Romans warns about worshiping the creation
rather than God the Creator: *Although they claimed to be wise,
they became fools and exchanged the glory of the immortal
God for images made to look like a mortal human being and
birds and animals and reptiles...They exchanged the truth
about God for a lie, and worshiped and served created things
rather than the Creator – who is forever praised.* (Romans
1:22,23,25) While some religions have actual idols that are
fashioned in the form of humans or animals, there are other
ways to elevate the creation over God. I could seek peace in
beautiful scenery, yet fail to acknowledge God. Someone else
might serve created things by pouring the majority of their time
and energy into pursuits relating to plants, animals, (or even
minerals) to such a degree that they have no space in their
schedule, mind or heart to reflect upon God.

Blessing and joy is found in worshiping and drawing close
to the Creator of the universe! *This is what God the LORD
says – the Creator of the heavens... who gives breath to its
people... "I the LORD, have called you in righteousness; I will
take hold of your hand."* (Isaiah 42:5-6)

Prayer for Today:

Dear God, you are the great and mighty
Creator of all things. I am a tiny part of the
universe, yet you love me personally. May I
never honor or serve any part of your creation
above You. Amen.

64

My Duet Partner

"The virgin will conceive and give birth to a son, and they will call him Immanuel" (which means "God with us"). Matthew 1:23

Piano teachers will sometimes play duets with their beginning students at their early recitals. The student will play a simple melody while the teacher performs a much more complicated part with rich chords and sparkling arpeggios. The overall effect, if the young student can keep a consistent tempo alongside the instructor, is to upgrade the performance and encourage the novice.

What if your music instructor agreed, not just to join you in a recital duet, but to come live in your home, demonstrate daily how to practice, and show by example how to improve your physical and mental health in order to achieve your greatest potential? The sacrifices of your teacher would change the trajectory of your life.

The prophet Isaiah predicted the birth of the Messiah by stating, *Therefore the Lord himself will give you a sign: The virgin will conceive and give birth to a son, and will call him Immanuel.* (Isaiah 7:14). Matthew tells us that the meaning of the name Immanuel is *"God with us"* (Matthew 1:23) and makes it clear that Immanuel is Jesus. God has indeed come into our world and led by example. Not only did Jesus show us how to live, but he willingly died to take upon himself the penalty due us for our sin. *Christ died for our sins according to the Scriptures, that he was buried, that he was raised on the third day according to the Scriptures.* (1 Corinthians 15:3-4)

In addition to being a good example and a selfless sacrifice, Jesus is the holy third person of the Trinity, equal to God. He performed miracles that only God could do. He received the worship of men and did not refute it. He referred to himself using the title only reserved for God (angering those who saw this as blasphemy): *"Very truly I tell you,"* Jesus answered, *"before Abraham was born, I am!"* At this they picked up stones to stone him... (John 8:58-59).

Jesus performed many other signs in the presence of his disciples, which are not recorded in this book. But these are written that you may believe that Jesus is the Messiah, the Son of God, and that by believing you may have life in his name. (John 20:30-31)

It is the divine Lord over all creation who wishes to partner with us in life. What should our response be to this invitation? First, we should turn to Christ for forgiveness. Second, we should follow his example. Finally, we should always be aware of his greatness and divinity, never treating his words or work as an afterthought.

Prayer for Today:
Dear God, it is amazing that you care for me as an individual. Thank you for sending Jesus into the world to be my Savior and my guide. Amen.

Like an Angel

Praise him, all his angels; praise him, all his heavenly hosts.
Psalm 148:2

"She sings like an angel!" This comment is often overheard after the performance of a female singer with a particularly pure tone. What does the Bible actually say about angels?

– Angels swiftly carry out the will of God. *Praise the LORD, you his angels, you mighty ones who do his bidding, who obey his word.* (Psalm 103:20)

–They are active, even when we cannot perceive them. *Do not forget to show hospitality to strangers, for by so doing some people have shown hospitality to angels without knowing it.* (Hebrews 13:2)

– They are entrusted with particular tasks, such as ministering to people or delivering special messages. *But the angel said to them, "Do not be afraid. I bring you good news that will cause great joy for all the people. Today in the town of David, a Savior has been born to you; he is the Messiah, the Lord."* (Luke 2:10-11)

– Multitudes of angels declare the praises of God, now and forever.. *Then I looked and heard the voice of many angels, numbering thousands upon thousands, and ten thousand times ten thousand...In a loud voice they were saying: "Worthy is the Lamb, who was slain, to receive power and wealth and wisdom and strength and honor and glory and praise!"* (Revelation 5:11-12)

– We should never give angels more honor than God. *I fell down to worship at the feet of the angel who had been showing them to me. But he said to me, "Don't do that! I am a fellow servant with you ...Worship God!"* (Revelation 22: 8-9)

– Demons are fallen angels who were removed from heaven when they joined Lucifer in his rebellion against God. Demons understand many truths about God, yet still refuse to submit to the Almighty. *You believe that there is one God. Good! Even the demons believe that – and shudder.* (James 2:19)

What makes angels happy? The angels rejoiced when God created the world: *Where were you when I laid the earth's foundation? ... while the morning stars sang together and all the angels shouted for joy?* (Job 38: 4,7) Even more wonderful, the angels rejoice when someone turns to Christ for repentance. In his parable of the lost sheep, Jesus promises: ... *there will be more rejoicing in heaven over one sinner who repents than over ninety–nine righteous persons who do not need to repent.* (Luke 15:7) We can praise God in a way that even the angels cannot: *he set my feet on a rock and gave me a firm place to stand. He put a new song in my mouth, a hymn of praise to our God.* (Psalm 40:2)

Prayer for Today:

Dear God, I sing praises to you today. Thank you for setting my feet on a rock and for sending many words of truth and encouragement through the angels. Amen.

Captive Audience

After they had been severely flogged, they were thrown into prison, and the jailer was commanded to guard them carefully. When he received these orders, he put them in the inner cell and fastened their feet in the stocks. About midnight Paul and Silas were praying and singing hymns to God, and the other prisoners were listening to them.
Acts 16: 23-25

    Paul and Silas traveled to the city of Philippi in Macedonia after Paul received a vision of a Macedonian man begging for his help. Their time in Philippi begins well, with the conversion of Lydia and her household. But things deteriorate when Paul and Silas are unjustly accused of starting a riot. They are stripped, beaten, and put in a bare, dank prison cell, their feet fastened in chafing stocks. As they spend the midnight hour praying and singing hymns, the other prisoners are forced to listen. We aren't told if any of these prisoners become believers, but we do know that later in the evening, a miraculous earthquake occurs which opens the prison doors and loosens everyone's chains. The jailer runs in, ready to kill himself because he fears that all have escaped, but Paul reassures the jailer that every prisoner is present. (perhaps a greater miracle than the earthquake!) The jailer falls on his knees, ready to hear about the saving grace of Jesus. The next day, Paul and Silas are released from the prison.

Like Paul and Silas, we are sometimes called to start a new ministry or to befriend someone. When the results of this new outreach include negative experiences, we can be tempted to question the initial summons. Paul and Silas endured great hardship in Macedonia, but they responded with song and prayer.

In general, it's not helpful to assault unsuspecting people around you with religious songs. But when you are experiencing a difficult situation with others and have the opportunity to interact lovingly, don't hesitate to ask them if you may pray aloud, and look for ways to gracefully share your confidence in the goodness of God. Always send up silent prayers for wisdom before beginning spiritual conversations with your "captive audience", and be careful that your words and actions honor God as the situation unfolds.

Prayer for Today:

Dear God, give me an openness to reach out to
other individuals that you place in my life.
May all that I say and do be in the center of
your will for me, and may I be your channel
for grace. Amen.

Excess Leads to Loathing

One who is full loathes honey from the comb, but to the hungry even what is bitter tastes sweet. Proverbs 27:7

Fund raising chocolate bars...guaranteed to increase your waistline along with profits. We all received our box of candy bars with great intentions to sell them to our friends and neighbors (and excitement about eating one or two.) We soon realized that most of our friends were music friends who were also a part of the sale, so unloading an entire box of candy was going to be difficult. Not to mention our accountability for the bars that were abandoned in a car on a hot day and were no longer prism shaped...So of course, we ended up eating way too many chocolate bars. The sweet, chocolaty taste that we initially loved was no longer as enjoyable. At some point, we didn't want to smell, taste, or even think about chocolate!

So many areas of life follow this same pattern. The new acquaintance who at first seems witty eventually grows tiresome when the jokes and loud conversation intensify. Christmas tunes played nonstop in the shopping mall become irritating. Walking through a boutique filled with scented candles creates an urge to escape the strong aromas.

The Book of Proverbs has good advice about avoiding excess:

A gossip betrays a confidence; so avoid anyone who talks too much. (Proverbs 20:19)

Do not join those who drink too much wine or gorge themselves on meat. (Proverbs 23:20)

Seldom set foot in your neighbor's house – too much of you, and they will hate you. (Proverbs 25:17)

Keep falsehood and lies far from me; give me neither poverty nor riches, but give me only my daily bread. Otherwise, I many have too much and disown you and say, "Who is the LORD?" Or I may become poor and steal, and so dishonor the name of my God. (Proverbs 30:8-10)

As you begin your day today, consider areas of life in which you are prone to excess. Ask the Lord to make you aware of tendencies towards surplus conversation, hoarding of riches, infatuation with television programs or sports, or anything that makes life unbalanced or harms the way Christ is represented in your life. Strive to only be *overflowing with thankfulness* (Colossians 2:7) and *filled with the fruit of righteousness* (Philippians 1:11)

Prayer for Today:

Dear Lord, fill me with the fruit of
righteousness so that others can see you. Make
me so thankful that I overflow with gratitude.
In other areas, help me to be discerning so that
I can avoid excesses that would dishonor your
character and harm my relationships with
others. I need your wisdom and strength.
Amen.

A United Front

I appeal to you, brothers and sisters, in the name of our Lord Jesus Christ, that all of you agree with one another in what you say and that there be no divisions among you, but that you be perfectly united in mind and thought. 1 Corinthians 1:10

Do you have a love/hate relationship with concert attire? Perhaps you love the way it unifies the look of your group, but you hate the actual outfit chosen by your director. You can complain all you want to your fellow orchestra or choir members, but your opinion of the apparel is of no consequence. You have no choice but to wear the garments so that your ensemble will present a unified front. Try to focus on the positives: you won't have to agonize over what to wear, and the harmonized look means that any of your own physical features that you dislike will be less evident to the audience.

When church members choose to put aside some of their own personal preferences in order to work together, those outside the church see unity, rather than division. When we unite, the shortcomings of individuals are not as obvious, and Christ's name is not dishonored by open bickering. This doesn't mean that everyone has the same perspective on every issue, just that they are looking to God for wisdom as to the best course of action.

Paul penned his first letter to the Corinthian church at a time when it was divided over leadership. *One of you says, "I follow Paul", another, "I follow Apollos", another, "I follow Cephas", still another, "I follow Christ."* (1 Corinthians 1:12) Paul had to remind them of Christ's supremacy and urge them to unite in their words and even their thoughts.

When there is a church split, or when two individual believers cannot resolve a bitter argument, nonbelievers are skeptical of the veracity of our faith. For many people, their only view of Jesus is their view of his followers, and often it's not a positive picture.

So what characteristics can we cultivate that will lead to unity? Paul counsels: *I urge you to live a life worthy of the calling you have received. Be completely humble and gentle; be patient, bearing with one another in love. Make every effort to keep the unity of the Spirit through the bond of peace. There is one body and one Spirit, just as you were called to one hope when you were called; one Lord, one faith, one baptism, one God and Father of all.* (Ephesians 4:1-6) Humility, gentleness, patience, forbearance – these all take effort to achieve, along with the help of the Holy Spirit. We have the same Father over us all. Let's graciously work together.

Prayer for Today:

Dear God, I can find it hard to put aside my own preferences and opinions. May I not cling to them and disrupt the unity of my fellowship of believers. Help us to work together in joy. Amen

Tuning Under the Radar

"Who can hide in secret places so that I cannot see them?" declares the LORD. "Do not I fill heaven and earth?" declares the LORD.
Jeremiah 23:24

Tuning a timpani before a concert requires patience, a good ear, a tuning apparatus such as a pedal mechanism, and an accurate pitch reference, such as a tuning fork. But what about tuning a timpani during a performance? The percussionist knows that a section of music is fast approaching which requires that the pitch of the timpani be changed, so she begins to quietly and accurately make the needed alterations. It's vital that all of the adjustments be implemented "under the radar" to avoid calling the attention of the audience to what she is secretly trying to accomplish.

There are many occasions in life that lead to secrecy. Some are nothing to be ashamed of, such as planning a special surprise for a coworker. But in many situations, acting in secret is accompanied by feelings of guilt because we know that what we are doing is wrong. Our actions might be unhelpful to ourselves or others (sneaking those extra brownies or accepting a bribe), inappropriate (spreading gossip or watching trashy TV shows), or contrary to God's best plan for our lives (deceiving others by not telling the whole truth.)

Of course, any covert action that we perform is no secret to the omniscient God of the universe. *You have set our iniquities before you, our secret sins in the light of your presence.* (Psalm 90:8) Even our inward thoughts are known to God. *Whoever slanders their neighbor in secret, I will put to silence; whoever has haughty eyes and a proud heart, I will not tolerate.* (Psalm 101:5) *...he knows the secrets of the heart* (Psalm 44:21)

Jesus did instruct his followers to do certain things in secret. We are to pray, fast, and give our tithes and offerings in such a way that we are not outwardly proclaiming our piety before others. *But when you pray, go into your room, close the door and pray to your Father, who is unseen. Then your Father, who sees what is done in secret, will reward you.* (Matthew 6:6)

Confess your secrets to God. He knows them anyway. He is gracious and forgiving. *If we claim to be without sin, we deceive ourselves and the truth is not in us. If we confess our sins, he is faithful and just and will forgive us our sins and purify us from all unrighteousness.* (1 John 1:8-9)

Prayer for Today:

Dear God, make me aware of any heart
attitudes or actions that I would not continue in
if you were present in the room with me –
because you are. Forgive my sin and restore
me to righteousness. Amen.

Morning 'Till Night

It is good to praise the LORD and make music to your name, O Most High, proclaiming your love in the morning and your faithfulness at night, to the music of the ten–stringed lyre and the melody of the harp.
Psalm 92:1-3

Psalm 92 reminds us that musical praise to God is fitting at any time of the day or night. Many of us spend the first minutes of the day totally focused on dressing in a rush and getting some coffee, but the psalmist suggests that we give our attention to proclaiming God's love. When he refers to the Lord as O Most High, we know that the writer understands his position relative to God. He is just a tiny part of the immense universe, yet God loves him and desires a personal relationship with him. Meditating on this early in the day gives us reason to praise the Lord as we start our daily activities. *When I consider your heavens, the work of your fingers, the moon and the stars, which you have set in place, what is mankind that you are mindful of them, human beings that you care for them?* (Psalm 8: 3-4)

At evening time, we are to make music which proclaims the faithfulness of God. Even at the end of a difficult day, we will be able to look back and focus on some way in which God has proven himself faithful. Perhaps we can only cling to the fact that we have endured and that God has promised to work all things together for good in our lives. *And we know that in all things God works for the good of those who love him, who have been called according to his purpose.* (Romans 8:28) A more positive day will bring opportunities to recount specific examples of God's grace. *LORD, you are my God; I will exalt you and praise your name, for in perfect faithfulness you have done wonderful things, things planned long ago.* (Isaiah 25:1)

Love and faithfulness are linked together in a multitude of Scripture passages, especially in the Book of Psalms. The biblical authors want to emphasize that our God personally cares for us, and that He acts faithfully for our good:

- *for I have always been mindful of your unfailing love and have lived in reliance on your faithfulness.* (Psalm 26:3)
- *Your love, LORD, reaches to the heavens, your faithfulness to the skies.* (Psalm 36:5)
- *For the LORD is good and his love endures forever; his faithfulness continues through all generations.* (Psalm 100:5)

Tomorrow, when you rise, center your thoughts upon the great love that God has for you. When you head to sleep, focus on his wonderful faithfulness. Make music with your voice and with instruments, praising our awesome Lord.

Prayer for Today:

Dear God, you are mighty and holy. Thank you that you care for me and that you prove faithful to all who trust in you. Please remind me to reflect on these truths before, during, and after the rush of each day's activities. Amen.

Adulation

So when you give to the needy, do not announce it with trumpets, as the hypocrites do in the synagogues and on the streets, to be honored by others. Truly I tell you, they have received their reward in full.
Matthew 6:2

Decisions, decisions…should I try out for a solo part, knowing that along with the prospect of personal enjoyment and public adulation I will also experience added pressure and scrutiny? Or should I skip the audition, abandoning fame but insuring a much less stressful concert experience? If I'm convinced that I have the ability to do a great job with the solo, and if I can avoid the temptation to let the compliments of others go to my head, then I should probably pursue the solo, and maybe applause will follow.

What would elicit the "applause" of Jesus? When Christ lived on Earth, here are some of the actions and attitudes that earned the praise of the Lord:

- Listening to the teachings of Christ: …*a woman named Martha opened her home to him. She had a sister called Mary, who sat at the Lord's feet listening to what he said… "Martha, Martha," the Lord answered, "you are worried and upset about many things, but few things are needed–or indeed only one. Mary has chosen what is better, and it will not be taken away from her."* (Luke 10:38-39, 41-42)

- Sacrificial giving: *Truly I tell you, this poor widow has put more into the treasury than all the others. They all gave out of their wealth; but she, out of her poverty, put in everything – all she had to live on.* (Mark 12:43-44)

- Forgiving others: *For if you forgive other people when they sin against you, your heavenly Father will also forgive you.* (Matthew 6:14)

- Humility: *Blessed are the poor in spirit, for theirs is the kingdom of heaven.* (Matthew 5:3)

In contrast, Jesus condemned those individuals who made a show of outward religiosity. He stated that those persons had already earned the reward of man's praise (insinuating that God would not praise or reward hypocritical, overly visible religious words and behaviors.) *Truly I tell you, they have received their reward in full. But when you give to the needy, do not let your left hand know what your right hand is doing, so that your giving may be in secret. Then your Father, who sees what is done in secret, will reward you.* (Matthew 6:2-4)

Prayer for Today:

Dear Lord, may my goal be to please you alone. I hope to someday hear the words, "Well done, thou good and faithful servant." May I not seek the praise of others by showcasing religious service or generosity, and my I humbly use any talents you have given to me only for your glory. Amen.

Deep Feelings

In the same way, the Spirit helps us in our weakness. We do not know what we ought to pray for, but the Spirit himself intercedes for us through wordless groans. (Romans 8:26)

Opera allows for the intense feelings of the characters to be expressed by singers in a way that exceeds what mere spoken lines could convey. The melodic elements and the orchestral accompaniment greatly enhance the emotions of the scene. Many operas have intricate plot lines that center upon tragic romance or complex heroes. The beauty of the musical score, the skill of the singers, and the grandeur and acoustics of the concert hall all work together to create a musical experience that speaks deeply to our emotional state.

Have you ever been in such anguish or despair that you could not even express your sentiments in words? Perhaps you could do nothing but cry with wrenching sobs or sit in silence. At other times, you may have been seeking for wisdom in the midst of a perplexing situation, and you had no idea how to pray.

The Bible promises that the indwelling Holy Spirit will come to our aid in situations such as these. The Spirit, the third person of the Trinity, intercedes, or mediates for us. *We do not know what we ought to pray for, but the Spirit himself intercedes for us through wordless groans.* (Romans 8:26) Because God the Spirit knows our hearts intimately, the Spirit is able to pray on our behalf. The Spirit also knows the good and perfect will of God for our lives. *And he who searches our hearts knows the mind of the Spirit, because the Spirit intercedes for God's people in accordance with the will of God.* (Romans 8:27)

Immediately following these statements about the Spirit's intercession for us, we find one of the most precious promises in Scripture: *And we know that in all things God works for the good of those who love him, who have been called according to his purpose.* (Romans 8:28)

Prayer for Today:

Dear God, I know that your Holy Spirit indwells every believer. Thank you that the Spirit will intercede for me when I do not know how to pray, and thank you that you have promised to bring good from every situation in my life. Amen.

Tough Audience

Several days later Felix came with his wife Drusilla, who was Jewish. He sent for Paul and listened to him as he spoke about faith in Christ Jesus. As Paul talked about about righteousness, self-control and the judgment to come, Felix was afraid and said, "That's enough for now!." Acts 24:24-25

Some evenings, the audience just doesn't seem to respond. You can sing the same show tunes as the previous night, dance the same numbers, and deliver the same comedic lines, but for some reason the normal response just isn't there. By the time intermission rolls around, you wish you could just slip out the backstage door.

What if you had to face a tough audience almost every night of your show's run? The apathy would become discouraging. Now imagine that instead of applause or indifference, you encounter raw opposition. After a few such nights, you'd be tempted to find a new line of work.

The apostle Paul made three different missionary journeys throughout Asia and other parts of the known world of that day. He experienced flogging, survived a shipwreck, and more than once was left for dead. He preached in temples and in jail cells.

He spoke before peasants and kings. Paul continued on despite severe opposition because his life had been totally transformed by the risen Christ, who had appeared to him on the road to Damascus.

One of Paul's most interesting audiences was Felix, the governor of Judea. The Jewish religious leaders have accused Paul of stirring up riots and profaning the temple. After Paul respectfully counters their accusations, Felix defers Paul's case for another day and has him returned to prison.

Finally, Paul gets another audience with Felix. You might expect Paul to keep his comments vague in order to stay in Felix's good graces, but the Bible gives this account of their meeting: *He sent for Paul and listened to him as he spoke about faith in Christ Jesus. As Paul talked about righteousness, self–control and the judgment to come, Felix was afraid and said, "That's enough for now! You may leave. ...he was hoping that Paul would offer him a bribe, so he sent for him frequently and talked with him.* (Acts 24:24-26)

Ouch! Paul speaks the hard truth to Felix about his spiritual condition, and the result is that Felix feels anxious and sends Paul away. Paul never bribes Felix, despite having many other meetings with the governor over a period of two years. Yet Paul remains faithful to God and is given other opportunities to speak boldly to kings and religious leaders.

Prayer for Today:

Dear God, when I read the life of Paul, the criticisms that I encounter for my faith seem small in comparison. Empower me with strength, wisdom, and boldness in your service through your Holy Spirit. Amen.

Musicosis

Let the message of Christ dwell among you richly as you teach and admonish one another with all wisdom through psalms, hymns, and songs from the Spirit, singing to God with gratitude in your hearts.
Colossians 3:16

Are you afflicted with the incurable malady of musicosis? The most obvious symptom of this illness is the tendency to burst into song whenever another person makes a statement that reminds you of a familiar tune. For example:

My friend asks, "Are you sleeping?", so I begin to sing, "Are you sleeping, are you sleeping, Brother John? Brother John?"

A newscaster mentions a campsite in the Shenandoah Mountains, and I burst into "Oh Shenandoah...I long to see you...Away you rollin' river."

Another symptom of musicosis is that of constantly having a melody running through your conscious thoughts. If an annoying song gets lodged in your brain, you have to make a specific effort to replace it with another tune, because otherwise you will never be able to make the melody disappear.

What is the cure for musicosis, or would you even want a cure? Perhaps it's difficult for you to even imagine a life without constant streams of music flowing through your mind. In any case, you can be a prime contestant on music trivia shows! Every musician, no matter how serious their degree of musicosis, should have their heart filled with grateful songs as they go through the day, consciously choosing to be filled with songs of praise – especially those that are based on Scripture.

The third chapter of Colossians uses the metaphor of allowing the message of Christ to dwell among us, indicating that eternal truths can be a part of our personal identity, not just during specific times of worship. *"Let the message of Christ dwell among you richly..."* (Colossians. 3:16) To dwell means to live, to settle in a place.

This passage also mentions that psalms, hymns, and songs from the Spirit can be used to *"teach and admonish one another with all wisdom"* (Colossians. 3:16). It's not just children who benefit from having important truths presented in melodic form. Music is a joy to our hearts, an avenue for expressing praise and gratitude, and a way to enrich and teach others.

Prayer for Today:

Dear God, you created me with a mind and heart that constantly default to music. May I be filled with songs of truth, and may godly actions and attitudes flow out of these songs. Amen.

Out of the Mouths of Babes

The crowds that went ahead of him and those that followed shouted,
"Hosanna to the Son of David!" "Blessed is he who comes in the
name of the Lord!" Matthew 21:9

What's your favorite day in the liturgical calendar? Many
Christians would name Christmas Eve or Easter. In childhood,
I would have chosen Palm Sunday, because as a member of the
children's choir we had an exciting role. Proudly grasping
palm fronds and arrayed in white robes, we would march down
the center aisle of the church, singing, "Hosanna, loud
hosanna!" and then remaining at the front to sing a special
anthem. Part of the excitement came from being able to sing
an uplifting melody. Looking back, I realize that another
source of the joy came from the satisfaction of serving –
contributing in an important way to the worship service.

Children benefit greatly when they are given opportunities
to serve. Whether it is singing, handing out bulletins, sweeping
up after a potluck dinner, or praying ahead of the meeting for
hearts to be drawn closer to God, it is good for church leaders
to intentionally plan ways to involve young people in the life of
the church. Kids are not just cute entertainment during a
service, or even examples of how to joyfully praise the Lord.

They are individuals who can grow in joyful, responsible service to others.

Don't have kids? Empty nester? Thoughtfully look for small ways to encourage, involve, and mentor the children that God places in your sphere of influence.

"Let the little children come to me, and do not hinder them, for the kingdom of God belongs to such as these. Truly I tell you, anyone who will not receive the kingdom of God like a little child will never enter it" (Luke 18: 16-17)

Prayer for Today:

Dear God, You love the children, and you have given them joyful hearts to praise you and important roles in which to serve. Open my eyes to see how I can build up the faith of the little ones that you put in my path. Amen.

Guide Right

He also told them this parable: "Can the blind lead the blind? Will they not both fall into a pit?" Luke 6:39

The key to maintaining straight lines in a marching band routine or a parade performance is for each band member in a given row to unobtrusively glance to their right and line up with the individual next to them. Theoretically, in this way the entire row can remain aligned, but of course the important marcher at the right end position must be accurate in order for the "guide right" approach to work.

For many individuals, spiritual development is based on a handful of Bible verses, perhaps taken out of context, or on ideas they have heard that don't really have a scriptural basis. For example, many people would be surprised to learn that the phrase "God helps those who help themselves" is never actually stated in the Bible, (although a conscientious work ethic is praised.) "Money is the root of all evil" is also not in the Bible. The book of 1 Timothy instead states, *"For the love of money is a root of all kinds of evil. Some people, eager for money, have wandered from the faith and pierced themselves with many griefs."* (1 Timothy 6:10)

89

Like band members depending on inaccurate guides, those who don't carefully study the truths of Scripture can find themselves way out of line, doctrinally or experientially.

Even if we depend upon preachers and Bible study leaders (or devotional books like this one) for insight, if these are our primary source of spiritual input we miss the opportunity and privilege of reading God's Word for ourselves. We can also miss connections among the verses that we read. By prayerfully meditating on the Scriptures, we are directly choosing to ask God, *"Open my eyes that I may see wonderful things in your law."* (Psalm 119:18)

Prayer for Today:

Dear God, Thank you for giving me your Word, so that I can hear directly from you and understand more about your character and your will for my life. Strengthen my commitment and desire to learn from you, and may the truth of your Word saturate my thoughts and change my life. Amen.

Spontaneous, Overflowing Praise

When Pharaoh's horses, chariots and horsemen went into the sea, the LORD brought the waters of the sea back over them, but the Israelites walked through the sea on dry ground. Then Miriam the prophet, Aaron's sister, took a timbrel in her hand, and all the women followed her, with timbrels and dancing. Miriam sang to them: "Sing to the LORD for he is highly exalted. Both horse and driver he has hurled into the sea." Exodus 15:19-21

Musical theatre productions are filled with songs that range from evocative ballads to catchy melodies to uplifting show–stoppers. During each of these, the audience must willingly accept the rather unbelievable premise that otherwise normal human beings will spontaneously burst into song (and often dance!) in various situations of life. For all of us who love music, this assumption isn't that difficult to believe, because life events often activate musical memories or spark the creation of a new melody.

The psalms of David were intended to be sacred poems set to music. These psalms reflected the outpouring of David's soul in times of despair and times of joy. *Hear my cry, O God, listen to my prayer. From the ends of the earth I call to you, I call as my heart grows faint.* (Psalm 61:1-2) *LORD, our Lord, how majestic is your name in all the earth! You have set your glory in the heavens.* (Psalm 8:1)

Mary's Magnificat was an overflowing of praise to God upon hearing Elizabeth's confirmation that Mary would become the mother of the Messiah. Mary quotes many Old Testament verses in her song. *My soul glorifies the Lord and my spirit rejoices in God my Savior, for he has been mindful of the humble state of his servant. From now on all generations will call me blessed.* (Luke 1:46-48)

Miriam spontaneously sang and danced after the parting of the Red Sea and the destruction of the enemies of the Israelites as they fled from Egypt. *Sing to the LORD for he is highly exalted. Both horse and rider he has hurled into the sea.* (Exodus 15:21)

The more we learn about God through the reading of the Scriptures, the more our minds and hearts will be full of truth that will spill over into songs of extemporaneous worship.

Prayer for Today:

Dear Lord, in good times and bad, may my initial thought and impulse be to reach out to you. May my soul be consistently nourished by what my mind reads in your Word, so that it overflows with songs that honor and praise you. Amen.

First Chair

You believe that there is one God. Good! Even the demons believe that – and shudder. James 2:19
If you declare with your mouth, "Jesus is Lord," and believe in your heart that God raised him from the dead, you will be saved. Romans 10:9

It's always an honor to be selected as first chair of an orchestra section. But no matter what your chair assignment, unless you actually sit down in the chair, you haven't demonstrated that you truly believe that the chair will support your weight.

Spiritual faith is a similar matter. A person can believe in some detached capacity that Jesus is the son of God, sent into our world to pay the penalty for sins. But true saving faith involves making the detached belief personal, honestly repenting of my own sins, and trusting that Christ will forgive me and create a new life of forgiveness and discipleship. Jesus said, *Very truly I tell you, whoever hears my word and believes him who sent me has eternal life and will not be judged but has crossed over from death to life.* (John 5:24)

93

In the days and years following a faith decision, there will be times when you question whether you are still a child of God, still forgiven and loved. While it's good to ask for forgiveness when we realize that our thoughts, words, or deeds have not honored God, it's also important to remember that we are not to constantly live in fear that God will reject us. Our new covenant with God is based on what Christ has accomplished for us, and that is an unchanging, strong foundation that will support us, now and forever. So be encouraged!

I write these things to you who believe in the name of the Son of God so that you may know that you have eternal life. (1 John 5:13)

Jesus Christ is the same yesterday and today and forever. (Hebrews 13:8)

For I am convinced that neither death nor life, neither angels nor demons, neither the present nor the future, nor any powers, neither height nor depth, nor anything else in all creation, will be able to separate us from the love of God that is in Christ Jesus our Lord. (Romans 8:38-39)

Prayer for Today:

O loving and faithful God, I truly believe that
you sent your Son the Lord Jesus to take the
penalty for my sins. I admit that I have sinned,
and I accept your offer of forgiveness and new
life. I trust that from now on, I am forever
your child. Amen.

Film Scores

As soon as you hear the sound of the horn, flute, zither, lyre, harp, pipe and all kinds of music, you must fall down and worship the image of gold that King Nebuchadnezzar has set up. Daniel 3:5

Famous music from film scores will immediately elicit certain reactions. Your stomach will knot in fear when you hear the jarring melody that signals an approaching shark. You will smile or cheer when trumpets herald the return of your favorite space hero. In each case, you know what is coming next, and your body responds.

During the time of the Babylonian captivity, God's people were exiled in Babylon under the rule of King Nebuchadnezzar, including Daniel and his friends Shadrach, Meshach and Abednego. King Nebuchadnezzar understood the power of spectacle. After installing a huge idol on the plain of Dura, he planned a dedication ceremony. The guest list included *satraps, prefects, governors, advisers, treasurers, judges, magistrates and all the other provincial officials...* (Daniel 3:2) A veritable "Who's Who" of important people! But the king is not content to hobnob with the famous. He demands that everyone present immediately bow and worship the golden idol whenever a certain musical cue is played. "*As*

95

soon as you hear the sound of the horn, flute, zither, lyre, harp, pipe, and all kinds of music, you must fall down and worship the image of gold that King Nebuchadnezzar has set up. Whoever does not fall down and worship will immediately be thrown into a blazing furnace." (Daniel 3:5-6) Shadrach, Meshach and Abednego refused multiple times to participate in idol worship; thus they were condemned to the fiery furnace.

Before being thrown into the flames, the three men make a profound statement about the power and sovereignty of God: *If we are thrown into the blazing furnace, the God we serve is able to deliver us from it, and he will deliver us from Your Majesty's hand. But even if he does not, we want you to know, Your Majesty, that we will not serve your gods or worship the image of gold you have set up.* (Daniel 3:17-18) God in fact does rescue the men, and the miraculous nature of their deliverance has a profound effect on Nebuchadnezzar. *Then Nebuchadnezzar said, "Praise be to the God of Shadrach, Meshach and Abednego, who has sent his angel and rescued his servants!...no other god can save in this way."* (Daniel 3:28-29)

How encouraging to see God work in a seemingly impossible situation, and how challenging to see the example of these three men.

Prayer for Today:

Dear God, in whatever situation you place me today, help me to be faithful to you. You are mighty, and you care for me. For this I praise your holy name. Amen.

Triple Threat

I pray that your partnership with us in the faith may be effective in deepening your understanding of every good thing we share for the sake of Christ. Your love has given me great encouragement, because you, brother, have refreshed the hearts of the Lord's people.
Philemon 1: 6-7

In musical theatre, a person who can sing, dance, and act exceptionally well is called a "triple threat". Any casting director would love to discover an actor with three solid areas of excellence. Now consider this question: Would it be fair for members of a church congregation to expect their pastor to excel in every area that might possibly be needed in that role? Is it even possible for someone to be a great orator, wise counselor, gifted administrator, and perhaps, even a passable singer? Probably not. Yet this is often the expectation, along with a desire for other more tangential attributes such as a handsome appearance or the lack of quirky mannerisms.

The Bible has plenty to say about the qualities of spiritual leaders, but most of the hallmarks are related to character traits and spiritual maturity, rather than comprising a resume of job performance skills. *Since an overseer manages God's household, he must be blameless - not overbearing, not quick–*

*tempered, not given to drunkenness, not violent, not pursuing
dishonest gain. Rather, he must be hospitable, one who loves
what is good, who is self–controlled, upright, holy and
disciplined. He must hold firmly to the trustworthy message as
it has been taught, so that he can encourage others by sound
doctrine.* (Titus 1:7-9)

Since no human being is perfect, even one who is growing
in the grace and knowledge of the Lord Jesus, it is vitally
important that we pray for our spiritual leaders. Pastors
experience many kinds of stress, not the least of which is the
pressure of counseling those who are in very difficult situations
while maintaining confidentiality. They undergo temptation,
encounter criticism, feel weary, and endure discouragement, all
while living their lives before the watching eyes of many.
Paul entreated the Romans, *I urge you, brothers and sisters, by
our Lord Jesus Christ and by the love of the Spirit, to join me
in my struggle by praying to God for me.* (Romans 15:30)

If you currently have a church home, will you pray for your
pastor? If not, as you consider the sort of leader that you are
seeking, will you use the qualities in Scripture as your guide,
and pray for wisdom in your search?

Prayer for Today:

Dear God, forgive me when I expect others to
have a whole series of attributes that I don't
even have myself. May I only use the
guidelines of your Word to evaluate any
individual, including myself. Bless my
spiritual leaders with encouragement and
strength, and make them more like yourself
day by day. Amen.

A Renewed Appreciation

Immediately his mouth was opened and his tongue set free, and he began to speak, praising God. Luke 1:64

Have you ever had laryngitis before a choral concert? You rest your throat and frantically sip herbal tea, hoping that your voice will be restored. You also gain a renewed appreciation for the ability to sing well whenever you wish.

Luke 1 contains a fascinating account of an incident in the life of Zechariah, the father of John the Baptist. One day when Zechariah is serving his priestly duty in the temple, the angel Gabriel appears and makes a startling announcement. Zechariah's wife Elizabeth (who has been infertile all the years of their marriage) will conceive a son who will be filled with the Holy Spirit and will prepare the way for the coming Messiah. When Zechariah expresses his doubts, the angel tells Zechariah that he will be unable to speak until the birth of the child. Nine months of silence! Soon after John is born, God restores Zechariah's voice, and what does he do? Curse God for keeping him in a mute state for such a long period of time? No. Zechariah immediately prophesies in the power of God's Spirit, praising God for his goodness to Israel and predicting John's mission as the forerunner for Christ.

Praise be to the Lord, the God of Israel, because he has come to his people and redeemed them...to enable us to serve him without fear in holiness and righteousness before him all our days...you will go on before the Lord to prepare the way for him, to give his people the knowledge of salvation through the forgiveness of their sins...to shine on those living in darkness and in the shadow of death, to guide our feet into the path of peace. (Luke1:68, 74-77, 79)

Perhaps the months of silence have given Zechariah ample time to reflect upon the miraculous circumstances of his wife's pregnancy. Maybe he has replayed in his mind the many exciting pronouncements that Gabriel had made concerning his son. *He will be a joy and delight to you, and many will rejoice because of his birth, for he will be great in the sight of the Lord...He will bring back many of the people of Israel to the Lord their God.* (Luke 1:14-16) Certainly he has learned patience, wisdom, and contentment through the long months of silence. May we gain these same virtues when our lives seem to be put on hold for a period of time, and may our lips be filled with praise and thanksgiving whenever we have the opportunity.

Prayer for Today:

Dear God, you worked miraculously in the lives of Zechariah and Elizabeth. All your promises to them were fulfilled, and their son John was used by you in a special way. May I believe the promises in Scripture and praise you in the times of waiting. Amen.

Fret Not

Do not fret because of those who are evil or be envious of those who do wrong; for like the grass they will soon wither, like green plants they will soon die away. Psalm 37:1-2

Many stringed instruments, such as the violin, viola, and cello, have no frets as guide marks on the fingerboard. Although the absence of frets can initially make it more difficult to learn those instruments, this allows for nuanced tones, greater accuracy in tuning, and more intricate playing techniques.

The word *fret* is also a verb that means to worry or to chafe. When we find a situation or a person to be irritating or unjust, our normal response is to stress out. The problem makes its home in our mind and our emotions, creating long–term anxiety that wears away at our joy and tranquility.

Psalm 37 outlines reasons why we should not fret, and it provides strategies for avoiding stress and anger.

We should not fret because God's justice will always prevail in the end. Worrying and anger also pull us into the evil that we so despise. *Refrain from anger and turn from wrath; do not fret – it leads only to evil. For those who are evil will be destroyed, but those who hope in the LORD will inherit the land.* (Psalm 37:8-9)

God will always uphold us, and faithfulness to him yields blessing. Therefore, don't compare yourself to the wicked who seem to be prospering around you. *Better the little that the righteous have than the wealth of many wicked; for the power of the wicked will be broken, but the LORD upholds the righteous.* (Psalm 37:16-17)

Look to God and trust in him for your safety. Make God the source of your joy. *Trust in the LORD and do good; dwell in the land and enjoy safe pasture. Take delight in the LORD, and he will give you the desires of your heart.* (Psalm 37:3-4)

Remind yourself that God has his own timing. He will not be mocked. *Be still before the LORD and wait patiently for him; do not fret when people succeed in their ways, when they carry out their wicked schemes. A little while, and the wicked will be no more.* (Psalm 37:7,10)

Finally, seek God's wisdom as to how to handle the situation. Even if you have made mistakes, God can help you to know how to move forward. *The LORD makes firm the steps of the one who delights in him; though he may stumble, he will not fall, for the LORD upholds him with his hand.* (Psalm 37:23-24)

Prayer for Today:

Dear God, you are just and you are good. You know the situation perfectly that is causing me such stress and anger. Give me an eternal perspective and guidance. Amen.

All I Can Hear Are Flutes

Plans fail for lack of counsel, but with many advisers they succeed.
Proverbs 15:22

In January of 1973, my high school band, along with every other public high school band in Fairfax County, Virginia, was invited to be a part of the inaugural parade for the second term of President Richard Nixon. Billed as "The Bicentennial Band", this mass band included 1976 members to match the "Spirit of 76" theme of the parade, (based on the nation's upcoming bicentennial.) The band was so large that our one and only marching rehearsal was held on an old runway of a nearby military base. While marching along in the middle of a flute section of over 200 flutes, all I could hear was the sound of flutes, piccolos, and a bit of the percussion section that had wisely been placed in the center of the gigantic ensemble to keep us in tempo. A very isolated perspective, indeed!

Surrounding ourselves with people from a similar background, economic level, or even a specific worship style preference can be similarly isolating. If everyone that I interact with is just a reflection of myself, I can expect that my ideas and perspectives will constantly be affirmed, even if those ideas and perspectives are not the best or only way to view the world.

It can also be problematic to approach decisions by either making choices totally on my own or by only asking advice from a few select people that I expect will back up my initial thoughts. The Bible encourages us to seek input from many advisors. Of course, these advisors should be individuals who honor God and have a good knowledge of Scripture, but they don't have to approach life according to my familiar patterns. Sometimes it's really helpful to hear from someone who will help us to "think outside the box" and challenge us to join a different part of God's diverse band of humans.

Prayer for Today:

Dear God, it's so easy to believe that my way
of approaching decisions or navigating through
life is always the best. You have created such
an array of insights, personalities, and
experiences. Help me to humbly seek
honorable, helpful, and perhaps varied
viewpoints. May I listen and learn your will
for my life. Amen.

Curtain Call of Faith

Now faith is confidence in what we hope for and assurance about what we do not see. This is what the ancients were commended for.
Hebrews 11:1-2

The curtain call at the end of a production generally follows a certain order. First to be recognized with applause are the members of the stage crew and the pit orchestra. Next to take bows are chorus members, then the actors who have minor roles, and finally the "stars".

The "roll call of faith" in Hebrews 11 follows no such sequence, other than a chronological one. The writer describes worshippers of God throughout history who demonstrated their faith by specific actions: Abel, Noah, Abraham, Isaac, Jacob, Joseph, Moses, Rahab, Gideon, the list goes on and on. Then there are the unnamed individuals who passed through the Red Sea, shut the mouths of lions, endured torture and imprisonment , and lived in caves. The author describes them perfectly when he says, *the world was not worthy of them.* (Hebrews 11:38)

Most of us will never experience the type of persecution endured by those who were flogged, forced to live in holes in the ground, and were even sawed in two. (Yes, this is clearly stated in Hebrews 11:37.) So which beliefs and actions in these forty verses can we use as examples for our lives?

- We demonstrate faith when we believe that God created the universe. (v.3)
- We demonstrate faith when we heed God's warnings like Noah, who built the ark. (v.7)
- We demonstrate faith when we move forward in faith like Abraham, who left his home for the promised land. (v.8-10)
- We demonstrate faith when we look to the future that God has promised for us. (v.20-22)
- We demonstrate faith when we align ourselves with God's people, even when it brings mistreatment. (v.24-26)

Did any of these Biblical heroes receive applause or rewards? They did receive God's commendation, but few received earthly honors or vindication over their enemies. *These were all commended for their faith, yet none of them received what had been promised, since God had planned something better for us so that only together with us would they be made perfect.* (Hebrews 11:39-40) What is it that we will be experiencing along side these exemplars of the faith? Eternal life in the presence of the Father.

And without faith it is impossible to please God, because anyone who comes to him must believe that he exists and that he rewards those who earnestly seek him. (Hebrews 11:6) Knowing that God is pleased is all the applause we should need.

Prayer for Today:
Dear God, each hero of the faith was a real
person like me who had fears and struggles.
May I learn from their example and live by
faith. Amen.

Too Close for Comfort

Come near to God and he will come near to you. Wash your hands, you sinners, and purify your hearts, you double–minded.
James 4:8

The piccolo has the highest range of any woodwind instrument. It's important for piccolo players to have a good ear for pitch, as piccolos can easily sound out of tune, especially if several are playing at once, as in the famous ending to John Phillip Sousa's march *Stars and Stripes Forever*. The piccolo can sound light and playful, but the highest notes can sometimes be piercing. It's often recommended that piccolo players wear earplugs.

Now imagine driving down the highway while your middle school aged child practices her piccolo in order to complete the required minutes of homework practice on the way home from an out of town event. Definitely too close for comfort! On the other hand, it's a desirable goal to want to draw close to God. *But as for me, it is good to be near God. I have made the Sovereign LORD my refuge; I will tell of all your deeds.* (Psalm 73:28)

We know that God, like the father of the prodigal son, is always watching and waiting for us to come to Him. So what is needed on our part in order for us to develop a closer relationship to God? First, be sure that you have asked for forgiveness. *But your iniquities have separated you from your God; your sins have hidden his face from you...* (Isaiah 59:2) *For God so loved the world that he gave his one and only Son, that whoever believes in him shall not perish but have eternal life.* (John 3:16)

Next, read and meditate in the Bible to learn how to more closely follow Christ. *Watch your life and doctrine closely. Persevere in them, because if you do, you will save both yourself and your hearers.* (1 Timothy 4:16) *These are the ones I look on with favor: those who are humble and contrite in spirit, and who tremble at my word.* (Isaiah 66:2)

Other ways to stay close to God are to join with others in fellowship and to prayerfully start each day by asking the Lord to guide your thoughts and actions. The almighty Creator can never be totally comprehended by mortals, yet He desires an intimate relationship with us. This should never be taken for granted! Let us be sure to take advantage of this amazing privilege.

Prayer for Today:

Dear God, you are the high king over all. It is astonishing that you desire a close relationship with me. May I not be indifferent to your call upon my life. 1 want to learn more about you and follow you in sincerity and purity. Thank you for your incredible love for me. Amen.

This Won't End Well

The LORD became angry with Solomon because his heart had turned away from the LORD, the God of Israel, who had appeared to him twice. 1 Kings 11:9

Solomon lived a life filled with numerous accomplishments. Rulers from around the world traveled to see his wealthy kingdom and listen to his great wisdom. He left a legacy of proverbs and songs that we benefit from today. God had even appeared to him twice.

Unfortunately, the end of Solomon's life was a disappointment. Solomon disobeyed the Lord by marrying foreign women – a LOT of foreign women. *He had seven hundred wives of royal birth and three hundred concubines, and his wives led him astray. As Solomon grew old, his wives turned his heart after other gods, and his heart was not fully devoted to the LORD his God...So the LORD said to Solomon, "...I will most certainly tear the kingdom away from you and give it to one of your subordinates.* (1 Kings 11:3-4,11)

If you look back at the earlier part of Solomon's life, you can detect a seed of the problem that would overtake him as he grew old. *Solomon made an alliance with Pharaoh king of Egypt and married his daughter. He brought her to the City of*

David until he finished building his palace and the temple of the LORD, and the wall around Jerusalem. The people, however, were still sacrificing at the high places, because a temple had not yet been built for the Name of the LORD. Solomon showed his love for the LORD by walking according to the instructions given him by his father David, except that he offered sacrifices and burned incense on the high places.
(1 Kings 3:1-2) Solomon makes two grave errors. First, he marries the daughter of Pharaoh, rather than a follower of the Lord. He will eventually have hundreds of wives and concubines. Second, he allows the people to mix pagan customs with the worship that God has outlined for them. The high places had formerly been used for pagan sacrifices, and blending the rituals will lead to many problems in the future.

It's more easy to slip away from God's best plan for our lives if we don't carefully examine our decisions to see if they agree with God's requirements. Like a loving parent, God's rules are designed for our own good throughout our lifetime.

Blessed is the one who does not walk in the counsel of the wicked, or stand in the way that sinners take or sit in the company of mockers; but whose delight is in the law of the LORD, and who meditates on his law day and night. That person is like a tree planted by streams of water which yields its fruit in season. (Psalm 1:1-3)

Prayer for Today:

Dear God, I don't want to fall away from you as I near the end of my life. I want to make wise and honorable choices now and through all my days. May your Word be my guide. Amen.

Uplifting Moment

But you, LORD, are a shield around me, my glory, the One who lifts my head high. Psalm 3:3

A Picardy third is a major chord that is placed at the end of a section of minor–key music. Some Picardy thirds are unexpected, while others are hinted at ahead of time by the composer. The effect of the Picardy third is a positive, uplifting feeling.

In the midst of dismaying, depressing times in our lives, we often feel that we need a heartening, encouraging moment. Psalm 3 was written by David during a time of extreme physical danger and emotional stress. His son Absalom was actually pursuing him with an army, looking to take his life. *LORD, how many are my foes! How many rise up against me! Many are saying of me, "God will not deliver him.".* (Psalm 3:1-2) Hopefully, most of us are not being physically chased by our own children, but there are countless other situations which cause us to cry out to God for deliverance. Based on David's experience, what are some ways that God can choose to send us our own encouraging "Picardy third"?

- God can calm our fears. *I lie down and sleep; I wake again, because the LORD sustains me. I will not fear though tens of thousands assail me on every side.* (Psalm 3:5-6)

- God can refute the taunts of those who mock God's role in our life. *Many are saying of me, "God will not deliver him." But you, LORD, are a shield around me, my glory, the One who lifts my head high. I call out to the LORD, and he answers me from his holy mountain.* (Psalm 3:2-4)

- God can change our circumstances. *Arise, LORD! Deliver me, my God!* (Psalm 3:7)

- God can send other blessings to uplift us. *May your blessing be on your people.* (Psalm 3:8)

Look to the Lord during your times of deepest distress and in moments when you just need a bit of a lift. His peace is a supernatural peace, and He has the ability to work all situations for your good. *Peace I leave with you; my peace I give you. I do not give to you as the world gives. Do not let your hearts be troubled and do not be afraid.* (John 14:27) *And we know that in all things God works for the good of those who love him, who have been called according to his purpose.* (Romans 8:28)

Prayer for Today:

Dear God, today I feel discouraged and need your help. Grant me your peace in this situation. May my actions and thoughts honor you in the midst of this troubling time. Please send deliverance and blessing, for my good and for your glory. Amen.

Recital Season

Preach the word; be prepared in season and out of season; correct, rebuke and encourage – with great patience and careful instruction.
2 Timothy 4:2

Accountants have tax season, quarterbacks have playoff season, and musicians have recital season. Actually, they have recital seasons, plural. December and May are jam packed with recitals, concerts, and other performances. If you are part of a musical family, it's "all hands on deck" as you take turns supporting one another.

The apostle Paul encouraged his young coworker Timothy to *be prepared in season and out of season* (2 Timothy 4:2) Timothy is to be prepared to share the Good News of Christ at all times, not only during the most convenient or opportune seasons of life. The same is true for us.

Timothy's preparation, to a great degree, has been secured through his mentoring relationship with Paul. During Paul's busy years of ministry, he has demonstrated how to faithfully follow the Lord in times of encouraging fellowship and in times of dangerous opposition. Paul referred to Timothy as *my true son in the faith* (1 Timothy 1:2), and they have had many opportunities to work together. Paul also encouraged Timothy to remember the godly heritage passed on from his grandmother and mother, as well as reminding him of the prophesies regarding his ministry.

In the same chapter, Paul tells Timothy that his own life is coming near to its end. *...the time for my departure is near. I have fought the good fight, I have finished the race, I have kept the faith. Now there is in store for me the crown of righteousness, which the Lord, the righteous Judge, will award to me on that day – and not only to me, but also to all who have longed for his appearing.* (2 Timothy 4:6-8) Paul is in the winter of his life, but he looks forward to a crown of righteousness. because has kept the faith and eagerly awaits the second appearing of Jesus. Paul's righteous status is based on his faith in Christ, rather than by his own efforts. *For in the gospel the righteousness of God is revealed – a righteousness that is by faith from first to last...*(Romans 1:17)

From the example of Paul, we learn that the end of life does not have to be a season to be feared. We can know that our sins have been forgiven if we believe in Christ's saving work on our behalf. We can look back on our days with satisfaction if we have participated in fruitful ministry through varied seasons of life. And we can have hope for the future if we have made a special effort to pass on our faith to the generation that follows.

Prayer for Today:

Dear God, is there someone that you are
calling me to invest my life in? Show me ways
to honor you during the time that we have
together so that they may always be ready to
serve you in season and out of season. Amen.

Love's Pure Light

You are the light of the world. A town built on a hill cannot be hidden. Neither do people light a lamp and put it under a bowl. Instead they put it on its stand, and it gives light to everyone in the house. Matthew 5:15

The most peaceful, magical part of a Christmas Eve service is the moment when the individual candles of the congregants are lit and everyone sings *Silent Night* a cappella. Little children solemnly grip their candles, excited about the rare chance to oversee a burning flame. Adults look around at the faces of their family members, illuminated by the golden glow. Harmonies blend and echo throughout the building. The words of the carol encourage our hearts:

Silent Night, holy night
Son of God, love's pure light.
Radiant beams from Thy holy face
With the dawn of redeeming grace
Jesus, Lord at thy birth
Jesus, Lord at thy birth

Jesus said "I am the light of the world." He also said, "You are the light of the world." The two statements are connected.

Jesus is the light because he is sinless purity. Only light can cause darkness to vanish. *I am the light of the world, Whoever follows me will never walk in darkness, but will have the light of life. (John 8:12)*

We are the light because we reflect the light of Christ, shining in a dark world. *You are the light of the world. A town built on a hill cannot be hidden. Neither do people light a lamp and put it under a bowl. Instead they put it on its stand, and it gives light to everyone in the house. In the same way, let your light shine before others, that they may see your good deeds and glorify your Father in heaven.* (Matthew 5:14-16)

Jesus is the light of life, the holy third person of the Trinity, our Creator and Redeemer. *In the beginning was the Word, and the Word was with God, and the Word was God. He was with God in the beginning. Through him all things were made; without him nothing was made that has been made. In him was life, and that life was the light of all mankind. The light shines in the darkness, and the darkness has not overcome it.* (John 1:1-4)

Prayer for Today:

Dear God, you are the light of life, and you were Lord even at your birth. I worship and praise you. Amen.

Called by the Composer

For it is by grace you have been saved, through faith – and this is not from yourselves, it is the gift of God – not by works, so that no one can boast. Ephesians 2:8-9

What an honor it would be to receive a specific invitation to join a prestigious symphony or chorale on the basis of talent! If your invitation came because you personally knew the conductor, the call to join would hold less prestige, but perhaps you would eventually be able to demonstrate that you had enough talent to justify the summons.

Now imagine that a famous composer grants an open invitation to anyone who would like to participate in a group that will enjoy one–on–one access to training by the great musician. All participants will also have the opportunity to perform uplifting, exhilarating music penned and conducted by that same composer. Your ability to play or sing the music perfectly at the first rehearsal will not be a requirement, just a willingness to set aside improper technique and totally depend on the life–changing advice of your esteemed leader. Would you jump at the chance?

The Bible teaches that no human has the moral purity or wholehearted reverence for God to qualify us for entrance into heaven. God reaches out to us with an offer of forgiveness that is available because Jesus absorbed the punishment of God on our behalf by his death on the cross. This offer is for everyone who will turn aside from sin and believe the good news of salvation. *"This righteousness is given through faith in Jesus Christ to all who believe. There is no difference between Jew and Gentile, for all have sinned and fall short of the glory of God, and all are justified freely by his grace through the redemption that came by Christ Jesus"* (Romans 3:22-24) The composer of our life story invites us to a new life filled with forgiveness and purpose. He will teach us how to increase in holiness as we follow his instructions, and we will have the opportunity to join with other believers in joyful service. What a privilege to be called by the composer!

Prayer for Today:

Dear God, I know that I have fallen short of your glory. I thank you for the opportunity to be freely forgiven because of the redemption you offer through faith in Jesus. I want to follow Jesus, and I trust him to change my heart and my life. Amen.

Murphy's Law

You will keep in perfect peace those whose minds are steadfast, because they trust in you. Isaiah 26:3

The first tech rehearsal for a concert or show always seems to conform to the popular adage "Murphy's Law": *Anything that can go wrong, will go wrong.* Microphones have squawking feedback, spotlights don't appear on cue, and risers are shaky. Stress levels escalate as just about everyone begins to wonder if things will come together in time for the performance. Yet there are often a few individuals who are able to remain calm. Why? Some have an underlying confidence in the skills of the tech crew and performers, so they feel optimistic that the difficulties can be worked out. Others focus their minds on the tasks at hand, rather than letting their thoughts jump ahead to frightening scenarios of future disaster. Still others have gone through the process so many times that they just tell themselves, "Bad rehearsal, great performance."

As we encounter complex situations, tight timelines, and unexpected problems in life, how can we possibly stay serene? We can modify and use the same strategies which the "chill" people utilize at a tech rehearsal. First, we can remind ourselves that our confidence is in a mighty, dependable, and loving God. He is able to manipulate circumstances, change hearts, and send peace. *From the LORD comes deliverance.* (Psalm 3:8) *Lord, there is no one like you to help the powerless against the mighty. Help us, LORD our God, for we rely on you...* (2 Chronicles 14:11) *And we know that in all things God works for the good of those who love him, who have been called according to his purpose.* (Romans 8:28)

Next, we can focus our minds on whatever we can currently contribute to fix the situation, rather than obsessing about the future. *Therefore do not worry about tomorrow for tomorrow will worry about itself.* (Matthew 6:34) *Do not fret because of evildoers or be envious of the wicked, for the evildoer has no future hope, and the lamp of the wicked will be snuffed out.* (Proverbs 24:19-20) *You will keep in perfect peace those whose minds are steadfast, because they trust in you.* (Isaiah 26:3)

Finally, we can look back at times when the faithfulness of God has been evident to us in the past. *Not one word has failed of all the good promises he gave through his servant Moses.* (1 Kings 8:56) *...I have always been mindful of your unfailing love and have lived in reliance on your faithfulness.* (Psalm 26:3) *Because of the LORD's great love we are not consumed, for his compassions never fail. They are new every morning; great is your faithfulness.* (Lamentations 3:22-23)

Prayer for Today:

Dear Lord, you know my situation and all its complex issues. I need your peace and wisdom today. May I focus my mind on your faithfulness and your power. Please help me to trust you and to remain calm. Amen.

About the Author

Nancy Bell Kimsey is a lifelong musician whose experiences have ranged from school bands and musical theatre to community chorale and church worship team. She moved to North Carolina to attend Wake Forest University and remained in the Tar Heel State throughout her career as an educator. She is a contributing writer for a number of publications and the author of *Grace on a Rambling Road: Devotions for RV Travelers* and *Joy by a Roaring Campfire: Devotions for Campers.*

CPSIA information can be obtained
at www.ICGtesting.com
Printed in the USA
JSHW011637170323
39081JS00003B/182

9 781736 773154